Oxford University Press, Walton Street, Oxford OX2 6DP

OXFORD LONDON GLASGOW
NEW YORK TORONTO MELBOURNE WELLINGTON
KUALA LUMPUR SINGAPORE HONG KONG TOKYO
DELHI BOMBAY CALCUTTA MADRAS KARACHI
NAIROBI DAR ES SALAAM CAPE TOWN

ISBN 0 19 432541 5

© OXFORD UNIVERSITY PRESS, 1965

First published 1965
Reprinted 1966 and 1967
Reset and reprinted 1969
Twelfth impression 1980

First Korean impression 1985
Second Korean impression 1993

Illustrated by DENNIS MALLET, MSIA

Printed in Korea

Elementary Stories for Reproduction 1

First Series

L. A. HILL

Oxford University Press

外 國 語 研 修 社

영어의 표현력 및 이해력 양성에 역점을 둔 L.A.HILL 박사의
명저 Stories for Reproduction 총서 한국판을 내놓으면서

우리의 국력이 크게 신장되어 국제 교류의 폭이 확대되어 감에 따라 각계 각층에서 영어에 능통한 인재의 요구가 날로 늘어가고 있습니다. 그러나 이러한 실력을 갖춘 인재는 구하기가 쉽지 않을 뿐 아니라, 최고 학부를 나온 분들 마저 영어를 필요로 하는 업무에 부닥치면 표현력(말과 글로 표현하기)이나 이해력(읽거나 듣고 이해하기) 부족 때문에 많은 곤란을 겪고 있습니다.

따지고 보면 이러한 현상이 생기게 된 것은 당연한 결과라고 할 수 있겠읍니다. 왜냐하면 지금까지의 영어 교육이 난해한 영문의 국역이나 까다로운 문법체계의 학습에 치중한 나머지 작문력, 회화력, 독해력 특히 속독력 및 청해력 등을 양성하는 학습을 소홀히 해 왔기 때문입니다.

그렇다면 영어의 표현력과 이해력을 기르기 위해서는 무엇부터 시작하여 어떻게 해야 하는지 그 구체적인 방법을 살펴 보기로 합시다.

1. 상용 2000 단어의 철저한 학습과 활용

영어로 일상적인 의사표시를 하는 데 있어서는 빈도수가 높은 것만을 뽑아 만든 2,000 상용 단어만의 사용으로 부족함이 없읍니다. 예를 들면 6만의 표제어와 6만 9천의 예문을 싣고 있는 Longman Dictionary of Contemporary English는 표제어의 정의와 그 예문을 제시하는 데 2,000의 「정의 어휘(Defining Vocabulary)」와 단순한 문법구조만을 쓰고 있으며, Longman Dictionary of Business English도 Michael West 의 상용 영어 단어 일람표(A General Service List of English Words)를 토대로 한 2,000여 단어와 단순한 문법구조만으로 Business 각 분야의 전문용어를 완벽하게 해설하고 있읍니다.

이런 사실만을 보아도 영어 실력 양성에 있어서 2,000 상용 단어의 철저한 학습과 그 활용연습이 얼마나 중요한 것이라는 것을 쉽게 이해할 수 있을 것입니다.

그럼에도 불구하고 이 2,000 상용 단어의 철저한 기초학습이 채 끝나기도 전에, 일상적 의사표시에는 별로 쓰이지 않아 기억하기도 힘든 많은 어려운 영어 단어들(고교 수준에서는 약 5,000, 대학과 대학원 수준에서는 10,000~30,000단어)을 단편적, 기계적으로 암기하거나 난해한 영문의 국역이나 까다로운 문법체계의 학습에만 매달린다면 아무리 노력을 해 봤자 모래 위에 성을 쌓는 격이어서, 영어로 자신의 생각을 자유롭게 표현할 수 있는 정도까지 그 실력이 향상되기를 기대할 수 없는 것입니다.

2. 문맥적 접근법(Contextualized Approach)

어학의 습득은 「의미내용」의 「기억, 재현」과정을 통해 이루어지는 것이며, 이 「의미내용」을 전달하는 효율은 1. 숫자(Figure) 2. 문자(Letter) 3. 단어(Word) 4. 문(Sentence) 5. 문장의 절(Paragraph) 순으로, 그것이 함축하는 「의미내용」의 차원이 높은 것일수록 그 전달량이 커지고 전달 효율이 높아집니다. 따라서 영어 학습에 있어서도 단어나 문법을 따로 학습하는 것보다는 문장내에서 문맥(Context)에 따라 이를 학습하는 것이 그 기억과 재현의 효율을 높일 수 있는 것입니다.

3. 표현력 향상을 위한 재현(Reproduction)연습

영어의 표현력을 기르는 데는 모범적인 영어 문장을 되풀이해서 읽고 이것을 재현(Reproduction)하는 연습을 해 보는 것이 가장 효과적이라는 것은 이미 널리 알려진 사실입니다. 그래서 중·고교의 교과서를 한 권이라도 암기해 보라고 권유하는 분들이 많으나, 이 교과서 자체가 암기와 재현 연습용으로 쓰기에는, 본문의 길이가 너무 길거나 난해할 뿐 아니라 재현 연습을 유도하는 적절한 Questions, Exercises 및 Answer Key 등의 뒷받침이 되어 있지 않기 때문에 표현력 향상을 위한 교재로는 적합하지 못합니다.

영어 교육계의 오랜 경험에서 밝혀진 바에 의하면 표현력 양성을 목적으로 하는 영어 문장 재현 연습용의 교재는 다음과 같은 요건을 갖춘 것이 가장 효과가 높다는 것입니다.

첫째 교재 본문의 내용이 학습자의 지속적인 흥미와 관심을 끌 수 있을 만큼 재미 있으면서도 교육적 가치가 풍부한 것이어야 하며,

둘째 교재에 사용되는 단어, 숙어, 문법구조등이 각 학습단계(입문, 초급, 중급, 상급수준 등)에 꼭 알맞게 제한 사용되어야 하며,

셋째 재현 연습에 쓰일 본문의 길이도 기억과 재현에 알맞는 단어수(학습 단계에 따라 150 단어 내지 350 단어의 길이)를 초과하지 않아야 하고,

넷째 학습시키고자 하는 단어, 숙어, 문법구조등이 교재의 본문에 흡수·통합되어 이것들이 각기 따로 따로 유리되어 있을 때보다 높은 차원의 「의미내용」을 갖도록 하여야 한다는 것입니다.

따라서 영어의 표현력과 이해력의 종합적인 향상을 위해서는 무엇보다 먼저 위에 열거한 네가지 요건을 갖춘 교재가 절대 필요한 것입니다. 그런데 이러한 교재의 입수가 지극히 어렵던 차에, 다행히 옥스포드대학출판부에서, 이 방면의 세계적 권위인인 L.A.HILL 박사로 하여금 위에 적은 네가지 요건을 모두 갖춘 영어 학습교재 총서를 저술케하여, 이를 최근에 모두 펴 내놓아 외국어로서 영어를 배우는 전세계 영어학도들의 절

찬을 받고 있는 것을 보고, 실용 영어의 통신 교육과 그에 부수되는 영어 교재의 출판을 전문으로 하고 있는 저희 外國語硏修社에서는, 이 교재의 한국내 출판이 저희들의 사업목적에 부합될 뿐 아니라 이러한 교재를 찾고 있는 수 많은 독자와 영어 교사들에게 크게 도움이 되리라고 생각하고 작년부터 옥스포드대학출판부와 판권 교섭을 해 오던 끝에 금년들어 계약이 성립되어 **L. A. HILL** 박사 저술의 영어 학습 교재중 **표현력 및 이해력 향상**에 역점을 둔 교재 전 **4** 집을 아래와 같이 내놓게 되었습니다.

제1집 **Stories for Reproduction 1** : 입문편, 초급편, 중급편 및 상급편의 Text 각
　　　　1권과 그 Study Guide(학습안내서)각 1권 및 이에 딸린 음성교재용 녹음테이프.

제2집 **Stories for Reproduction 2** : 입문편, 초급편, 중급편 및 상급편의 Text 각
　　　　1권과 그 Answer Key 각 1권 및 이에 딸린 음성교재용 녹음테이프.

제3집 **Steps to Understanding** : 입문편, 초급편, 중급편 및 상급편의 Text 각 1권
　　　　과 그 Answer Key 각 1권 및 이에 딸린 음성교재용 녹음테이프.

제4집 **Stories for Reproduction** (American Series) : 초급편, 중급편 및 상급편의
　　　　Text 각 1권과 그 **Answer Key** 및 이에 딸린 음성교재용 녹음테이프.

　전 세계적인 Best Seller 가 되어 있는 이 교재는 표현력과 독해력 향상에 필수적인 단어·숙어와 문법구조를 4 단계로 나누어 제한 사용하고 있어 독자들에게 학습상의 부담을 주지 않을 뿐 아니라 그 본문이 유우머(해학)와 윗트(기지)로 가득찬 흥미진진한 짧은 이야기로 되어 있기 때문에 그것을 끝까지 단숨에 읽을 수 있도록 되어 있으며, 이 이야기를 속독, 청취, 정독, 재청(再聽)한 다음 다양한 Questions와 Exercises 를 사용한 문답식 방법으로 그 내용을 이해하는 훈련을 쌓는 동시에 이를 다시 말과 글로 표현해 보는(Oral & Written Reproduction)연습을 되풀이 함으로써, 난해한 영문국역, 단편적인 단어·숙어의 암기나 문법체계의 학습등에서 오는 정신적 긴장과 피로를 수반하지 않고, 독자들이 이야기의 내용을 즐기다 보면 자기도 모르는 사이에 이해력과 표현력이 몸에 붙도록 꾸며져 있습니다.

　또한 이 교재는 Text와는 따로 **Study Guide**(학습안내서), **Answer Key** (해답집) 및 녹음테이프가 딸려 있어 개인의 자습(Self-Study)용으로는 물론 교실 수업용으로도 쓸 수 있도록 만들어져 있습니다.

　이 교재가 많은 독자들의 영어 표현력 및 이해력 향상에 획기적인 도움이 되기를 바랍니다.

1985년 1월 5일

外國語硏修社

代表理事
會　長　李　瀅　載

머 리 말

이 책은 재미 있고 읽기 쉬운 이야기를 이용하여 영어의 이해력(읽거나 듣고 이해하기)과 표현력(말이나 글로 나타내기)을 향상시킬 것을 목적으로 하고 있읍니다. 이 책은 그 초급편입니다. 입문편을 마친 분 또는 이와 동등한 실력이 있는 분은 이책을 이용하여 한층 더 높은 영어 실력을 쌓을 수 있도록 꾸며져 있읍니다.

구 성

이 책에는 150단어 길이로 쓰여진 이야기 56편이 담겨져 있으며 각 편마다 이야기의 내용을 말이나 글로 재현(Oral or Written Reproduction)하는 공부를 시키기 위한 질의문들이 따르고 있고 그 해답은 Study Guide(주해서)에 따로 실려 있읍니다.

이 책의 본문으로 쓰여진 이야기는 권말의 부록에 수록된 1,000 단어 범위 안에서 쓰여진 평이한 것이며 문법구조 또한 입문편보다는 약간 정도가 높으나 기초적인 수준으로 제한되어 있읍니다.

Study Guide와 음성교재

이 책에는 지도교사 없이 혼자서 자습하는 분들의 학습을 돕기 위하여 따로 Study Guide(주해서)가 마련되어 있읍니다. 이 Study Guide는 (1) 본문에 나오는 중요한 단어·숙어의 뜻, 발음 및 어법의 상세한 해설과 그 예문으로 이루어진 Notes, (2) 이야기의 요점을 적어놓은 Point of the Story와 (3) 이야기의 내용에 대한 질의문의 해답(Answers)으로 구성되어 있읍니다. 이 책의 질의문들에는 번호가 없으나 왼쪽 난부터 위에서 아래로 1, 2, 3…. 의 번호를 붙이면 Study Guide의 해답번호와 일치합니다.

이 교재에 딸려 있는 음성교재는 영국의 교양 있는 일류 성우가 표준영어를 사용하여 취입한 것으로 이야기 전문(全文)과 그 내용의 질의문이 재현 연습에 꼭 알맞도록 녹음되어 있어 영어의 청취력 및 회화력 향상을 위해서는 더할 나위 없이 적합한 교재입니다.

공부하는 방법

가정에서 지도교사의 도움 없이 자습하는 경우에는 먼저 녹음테이프로 본문의 이야기를 1～2회 들은 다음 책을 펴 보고 얼마나 정확하게 알아들었는지 확인해 봅니다. 만일 새로운 단어·숙어나 표현법이 있어 확실한 이해가 되지 않으면 Study Guide를 펴서 Notes를 참고하고 그래도 미심쩍으면 사전을 찾아 봅니다. 청해력에 자신이 없는 분들은 먼저 본문을 2～3회 읽고 난 후 대충 이해가 된 다음에 녹음테이프를 들어도 좋습니다. 이야기의 내용이 이해가 되면 이번에는 책을 덮고 그 내용을 되도록 많이 공책에 써서 재현해 본 다음 원문과 비교하여 틀린 곳을 바로잡아 가는 것이 대단히 중요합니다.

이야기 다음에는 그 내용을 순서대로 조금씩 재현시키기 위한 질문이 뒤따릅니다. 이 질문에 대한 답을 완전한 문장 형식으로 공책에 써 본 후 Study Guide의 해답과 대조해 보고 틀린 점을 바로잡습니다.

그 다음에는 테이프로 이야기를 2~3회 다시 들어 보고 질문을 들으면서 구두로 답을 해 본 후 Study Guide의 정답과 대조해 봅니다.

(2) 교실수업에 이용하는 경우 교실수업의 경우에는 이 교재를 다음과 같은 방법으로 이용할 수 있겠습니다.

(i) 청취 후 구두발표(Listening and Speaking)

선생님이 학생들에게 이야기를 2~3회 낭독해 주거나 녹음된 테이프로 이야기를 2~3회 들려 준 다음 그 내용을 구두로 재현하도록 하거나 이야기 다음에 나오는 질문에 구두로 답변하도록 합니다. 이 방법은 30인 이내의 적은 인원수일 경우에 가장 적합합니다.

(ii) 청취 후 다시 써 보기(Listening and Writing)

선생님이 학생들에게 이야기를 2~3회 낭독해 주거나 녹음된 테이프로 들려준 다음 기억해 낼 수 있는 최대한으로 이야기의 내용을 공책에 써 보도록 합니다. 그 다음에는 이야기에 대한 질문들을 받아 쓰게 하거나 칠판에 써 놓고 그 답을 공책에 써 보도록 합니다. 이 방법은 학생수가 50인 내외인 교실수업의 경우에 적합합니다.

(iii) 읽은 후 다시 써 보기(Reading and Writing)

학생들로 하여금 이야기를 되도록 많이 빠른 속도로 읽게 한 후 간단한 True or False Questions를 만들어 속독력을 평가해 봅니다. 다음에는 이야기를 2~3회 정독시킨 후 책을 덮고 이야기를 최대한으로 기억하여 공책에 써 보도록 하거나 이야기 다음에 나열된 질문들에 대한 답을 공책에 써 보도록 합니다.

(i) (ii) (iii) 어느 경우에나 이야기를 읽거나 듣는 것과 그 재현 사이에 며칠간의 간격을 두는 것이 경우에 따라서는 더욱 효과적일 수도 있습니다.

L. A. Hill 박사가 1,000표제어 수준으로 쓴 교재에는 다음과 같은 것들이 있습니다.

Word Power 1500: Vocabulary Tests and Exercises in American English

Elementary Stories for Reproduction, Series 2

Elementary Stories for Reproduction, American Series

Elementary Steps to Understanding

Oxford Graded Reader, 1000-Headword Level: Junior and Senior Stories

Introduction

In his earlier series' of practice books*, Dr. Hill has used three levels, his elementary (1 000-headword), intermediate (1 500-headword) and advanced (2 075-headword) levels. In this new series, however, there is also another level, the introductory (750-headword) level. This book is at the 1 000-headword level.

Each story is about 150 words long, and some of the stories contain one or two words outside the grading. These are listed on the pages on which they appear, and can be looked up in a dictionary before work is begun. In the instructions for the exercises, the word 'false' is also outside the grading. In the exercises, 'puzzle' is too. All the levels are very carefully graded, and this covers not only vocabulary, but also idioms and grammar.

These four books are intended chiefly to help students read English more easily and with more comprehension, but they can also be used:

(i) for practice in understanding spoken English (with the student listening to the teacher, or to the cassette);

(ii) for practice in writing English (by answering the questions in English; by writing as much of the story as the student can remember; and by doing the exercises); and

(iii) for improving the student's command of vocabulary, idioms and grammar (again by doing certain of the exercises).

If the student wishes to use the books *only* for practice in reading comprehension, he/she should read a story and then answer questions *in his/her mother-tongue*.

He/She can also try reading some (or all) of the questions *first*, and then reading the story to find the answers to the questions before answering them. To increase speed of reading, the student can time himself/herself with a watch or clock, and try to read as fast as possible, *provided that he/she can still understand*.

Stories for Reproduction, Series 1 and 2 and *Elementary* and *Intermediate Comprehension Pieces*, all published by Oxford University Press.

Elementary Stories 1
for Reproduction

First Series

I

It was two weeks before Christmas, and Mrs Smith was very busy. She bought a lot of Christmas cards to send to her friends and to her husband's friends, and put them on the table in the living-room. Then, when her husband came home from work, she said to him, 'Here are the Christmas cards for our friends, and here are some stamps, a pen and our book of addresses. Will you please write the cards while I am cooking the dinner?'

Mr Smith did not say anything, but walked out of the living-room and went to his study. Mrs Smith was very angry with him, but did not say anything either.

Then a minute later he came back with a box full of Christmas cards. All of them had addresses and stamps on them.

'These are from last year,' he said. 'I forgot to post them.'

When was Mrs Smith very busy?
What did she do?
Why did she buy the cards?
Where did she put them?
What did she say to her husband?

What did Mr Smith say?
What did he do?
How did Mrs Smith feel?
What did she say?
What did Mr Smith do a minute later?
What did he say?

2

Mrs Jones was waiting for an important telephone call, but she had no bread in the house, so she left the baby at home and said to his five-year-old brother, 'I am going to the shops, Jimmy, and I will be back in a few minutes.'

While she was out, the telephone rang, and Jimmy answered. 'Hullo,' said a man, 'is your mother there?'

'No,' answered Jimmy.

'Well, when she comes back, say to her, "Mr Baker telephoned".'

'What?'

'Mr Baker. Write it down. B-A-K-E-R.'

'How do you make a B?'

'How do I make . . .? Listen, little boy, is there anybody else with you? Any brothers or sisters?'

'My brother Billy is here.'

'Good, I want to talk to him, please.'

'All right.' Jimmy took the telephone to the baby's bed and gave it to Billy. When their mother came back, she asked, 'Did anyone telephone?'

'Yes,' said Jimmy, 'a man. But he only wanted to talk to Billy.'

What was Mrs Jones waiting for?
Why did she go out?
What did she do with the baby when she went out?
What did she say to Jimmy?
How old was he?
What happened while she was out?
What did Jimmy do?
What did the man say?
What did Jimmy answer?

What did the man say then?
What did Jimmy say?
What was the man's answer?
What did Jimmy ask him then?
What did the man say then?
What did Jimmy answer?
What did the man say?
What did Jimmy say?
What did he do?
What did Jimmy's mother do when she came home?
What did Jimmy answer?

3

Nasreddin* had an old shed. It had no windows, so it was very dark, and it was full of old things.

One day Nasreddin went into this shed to get a ladder, but slipped on something and fell against a big garden fork. The fork hit him on the head and knocked him down. Then it fell on top of him and hit him hard on the left leg. The ends of the fork then went into his long beard. He fought with the fork fiercely, and at last threw it off him, jumped up and ran out of the shed. He was very angry. He had an old sword under his bed, and he now ran and got this. Then he ran back to the shed, opened the door suddenly and shouted in a terrible voice, 'All right, come out and fight, you and all the other forks in the world! I'm not afraid of you!'

* Pronounced /nʌsredˈdiːn/ (*nuss*, to rhyme with *bus*; *red*; *deen*, to rhyme with *seen*. The stress is on the last syllable).

What did Nasreddin have?	What did it do after that?
What was it like inside?	What did the ends of the fork do?
Why was it dark?	
What happened one day?	What did Nasreddin do?
Why did Nasreddin go into the shed?	How did he feel?
	What did he have under his bed?
What did he do inside the shed?	What did he do now?
What did the fork do?	What did he shout?

6

4

A man always went to the same bar at the same time every day and asked for two glasses of beer. He drank them and then asked for two more.

One day the man behind the bar said to him, 'Why do you always ask for two glasses of beer? Why don't you get one big glass instead?'

The man answered, 'Because I do not like to drink alone. I drink with my friend.'

But a few days later the man came in and asked only for one beer.

'Oh,' said the barman, 'has your friend died?'

'Oh, no,' said the man. 'He is very well. This beer is for him. But I have stopped drinking beer. My doctor doesn't want me to drink any more because it is dangerous for me.'

What did the man in this story do every day?
What did he ask for?
What did he do then?
What did the man behind the bar say one day?
What did the man answer?

What happened a few days later?
What did the man ask for this time?
What did the barman ask?
What did the man answer?

5

Old Mr Black loved shooting bears, but his eyes were not good any more. Several times he nearly shot people instead of bears, so his friends were always very careful when they went out shooting with him.

One day a young friend of his wanted to have a joke, so he got a big piece of white paper and wrote on it in very big letters 'I AM NOT A BEAR'. Then he tied it to his back and went off. His friends saw it and laughed a lot.

But it did not save him. After a few minutes Mr Black shot at him and knocked his hat off.

The young man was frightened and angry. 'Didn't you see this piece of paper?' he shouted to Mr Black. 'Yes, I did,' said Mr Black. Then he went nearer, looked carefully at the paper and said, 'Oh, I am very sorry. I did not see the word NOT.'

What did Mr Black love?
What was the matter with him?
What happened several times?
What did his friends do when they went out shooting with him?
What did one of his young friends want to do one day?
What did he do?
What did he write on the piece of paper?

What did he do then?
What did his friends do?
What happened then?
Did the paper save the young man?
How did he feel?
What did he shout?
What did Mr Black do?
What did he say?

6

Mrs Brown's old grandfather lived with her and her husband. Every morning he went for a walk in the park and came home at half past twelve for his lunch.

But one morning a police car stopped outside Mrs Brown's house at twelve o'clock, and two policemen helped Mr Brown to get out One of them said to Mrs Brown, 'The poor old gentleman lost his way in the park and telephoned us for help, so we sent a car to bring him home.' Mrs Brown was very surprised, but she thanked the policemen and they left.

'But, Grandfather,' she then said, 'you have been to that park nearly every day for twenty years. How did you lose your way there?'

The old man smiled, closed one eye and said, 'I didn't quite lose my way. I just got tired and I didn't want to walk home!'

Who lived with Mr and Mrs Brown?
What did he do every morning?
When did he come home?
What did he come home for?
What happened one morning?
At what time did it happen?
What did the two policemen do?

What did one of them say to Mrs Brown?
How did Mrs Brown feel?
What did she do?
What did she say to her grandfather?
What did the old man do?
What did he say?

7

Helen's eyes were not very good, so she usually wore glasses. But when she was seventeen and she began to go out with a young man, she never wore her glasses when she was with him. When he came to the door to take her out, she took her glasses off, and when she came home again and he left, she put them on.

One day her mother said to her, 'But Helen, why do you never wear your glasses when you are with Jim? He takes you to beautiful places in his car, but you don't see anything.'

'Well, Mother,' said Helen, 'I look prettier to Jim when I am not wearing my glasses—and he looks better to me too!'

What did Helen usually wear?
Why did she do this?
What did she begin to do when she was seventeen?
What did she do when she was with the young man?
Why did the young man come to the door?

What did Helen do then?
What did she do when she came home?
What did her mother say to her one day?
What did Helen answer?

8

A man was trying to build an electric motor-car. He worked in an office in the town during most of the week, but on Saturdays and Sundays he stayed at home in the country and worked on his electric car. Every Monday he told his friends at the office about his work on the car, but his news about it was never very good. Then at last one Monday morning he came to the office and said to his friends, 'I have done it! I have driven from my home to here by electricity!'

His friends were all very glad. 'How much did it cost to get here by electricity?' they asked.

'Three hundred and two pounds,' he answered. 'Two pounds for the electricity, and three hundred pounds for the electric wires from my house to the car.'

What was the man in this story trying to do?	What was his news about the car like?
What did he do most of the week?	What happened at last one Monday morning?
What did he do on Saturdays and Sundays?	How did his friends feel?
	What did they say?
What did he do every Monday?	What did the man answer?

9

An artist went to a beautiful part of the country for a holiday, and stayed with a farmer. Every day he went out with his paints and his brushes and painted from morning to evening, and then when it got dark, he went back to the farm and had a good dinner before he went to bed.

At the end of his holiday he wanted to pay the farmer, but the farmer said, 'No, I do not want money—but give me one of your pictures. What is money? In a week it will all be finished, but your painting will still be here.'

The artist was very pleased and thanked the farmer for saying such kind things about his paintings.

The farmer smiled and answered, 'It is not that. I have a son in London. He wants to become an artist. When he comes here next month, I will show him your picture, and then he will not want to be an artist any more, I think.'

Where did the artist go for his holiday?

Where did he stay?

What did he do every day?

What did he do when it got dark?

What did the farmer say when the artist wanted to pay him?

What did the painter thank the farmer for?

Why did the farmer want the artist's painting?

Did the farmer want his son to become an artist?

10

Mr Jones was very angry with his wife, and she was very angry with her husband. For several days they did not speak to each other at all. One evening Mr Jones was very tired when he came back from work, so he went to bed soon after dinner. Of course, he did not say anything to Mrs Jones before he went upstairs. Mrs Jones washed the dinner things and then did some sewing. When she went up to bed much later than her husband, she found a piece of paper on the small table near her bed. On it were the words, 'Mother.—Wake me up at 7 a.m.—Father.'

When Mr Jones woke up the next morning, it was nearly 8 a.m.—and on the small table near his bed he saw another piece of paper. He took it and read these words: 'Father.—Wake up. It is 7 a.m.—Mother.'

Why did Mr and Mrs Jones not speak to each other for several days?

Why did Mr Jones go to bed soon after dinner?

Did he speak to his wife before he went upstairs?

What did Mrs Jones do after dinner?

When did she go to bed?

What did she find when she went to bed?

Where did she find it?

What did she read?

At what time did Mr Jones wake up the next morning?

What did he see when he woke up?

What did he read?

Why did Mr Jones not wake up at 7 a.m.?

11

The lights were red, so the old man stopped his car and waited for them to change to green. While he was waiting, a police car came up behind him, hit his car hard in the back and stopped.

There were two policemen in the police car, and they were very surprised and glad when the old man got out of his car and walked towards them without any trouble after such an accident. He was over 70 years old.

The old man came to the door of the police car, smiled kindly, and said, 'Tell me, young man, how do you stop this car when the lights are red and I am not here?'

Why did the old man stop his car?

What did he wait for?

What happened while he was waiting?

What people were there in the police car?

What did the old man do?

How did the policemen feel about it?

Why were they surprised?

How old was the man?

What did he do then?

What did he say?

12

Mrs Williams loved flowers and had a small but beautiful garden. In the summer, her roses were always the best in her street. One summer afternoon her bell rang, and when she went to the front door, she saw a small boy outside. He was about seven years old, and was holding a big bunch of beautiful roses in his hand.

'I am selling roses,' he said. 'Do you want any? They are quite cheap. Five pence for a big bunch. They are fresh. I picked them this afternoon.'

'My boy,' Mrs Williams answered, 'I pick roses whenever I want, and don't pay anything for them, because I have lots in my garden.'

'Oh, no, you haven't,' said the small boy. 'There aren't any roses in your garden—because they are here in my hand!'

What did Mrs Williams love?
What did she have?
What were her roses like in the summer?
What happened one summer afternoon?
What did Mrs Williams do then?
What did she see?
Where did she see this boy?

How old was he?
What was he holding?
What did he say to Mrs Williams?
What did Mrs Williams answer?
What did the small boy say then?
Why weren't there any roses in Mrs Williams's garden?

I3

A woman was having some trouble with her heart, so she went to see the doctor. He was a new doctor, and did not know her, so he first asked some questions, and one of them was, 'How old are you?'

'Well,' she answered, 'I don't remember, doctor, but I will try to think.' She thought for a minute and then said, 'Yes, I remember now, doctor! When I married, I was eighteen years old, and my husband was thirty. Now my husband is sixty, I know; and that is twice thirty. So I am twice eighteen. That is thirty-six, isn't it?'

Where did the woman in this story go?

Why did she go there?

Why did the doctor not know her?

What did he do first?

What was one of his questions?

What did the woman answer?

What did she do then?

What did she say after that?

How old was the woman *really*?

14

One day Mrs Jones went shopping. When her husband came home in the evening, she began to tell him about a beautiful cotton dress. 'I saw it in a shop this morning,' she said, 'and . . .'

'And you want to buy it,' said her husband. 'How much does it cost?'

'Fifteen pounds.'

'Fifteen pounds for a cotton dress? That is too much!'

But every evening, when Mr Jones came back from work, his wife continued to speak only about the dress, and at last, after a week, he said, 'Oh, buy the dress! Here is the money!' She was very happy.

But the next evening, when Mr Jones came home and asked, 'Have you got the famous dress?' she said, 'No.'

'Why not?' he said.

'Well, it was still in the window of the shop after a week so I thought, "Nobody else wants this dress, so I don't want it either".'

What did Mrs Jones do one day?

When did her husband come home?

What did Mrs Jones do when he came home?

What did she say to him?

What did he answer?

What did she say?

What did Mr Jones say then?

What happened every evening after that?

What happened after a week?

What did Mr Jones ask the next evening?

What did Mrs Jones answer?

What did her husband say then?

What was her answer?

15

One day a lady walked into a hat shop. The shopkeeper smiled and said, 'Good afternoon, madam.'

'Good afternoon,' the lady answered. 'There is a green hat with red flowers and blue leaves on it in your window. Will you please take it out of there.'

'Yes, madam,' the shopkeeper said. 'I will be very pleased to do that for you.' Usually ladies looked at a lot of hats before they chose one, and the shopkeeper got very tired. 'Good', he thought, 'I will sell this hat very quickly—and it has been in my window for a very long time.'

'Do you want it in a box, madam,' he asked, 'or will you wear it?'

'Oh, I don't want it,' she answered. 'I only wanted you to take it out of your window. I pass your shop every day, and I hate to see the ugly thing there!'

What happened one day?
What did the shopkeeper do?
What did he say?
What did the lady answer?
What did the shopkeeper say then?

What usually happened in the shop?
What did the shopkeeper think?
What did he say to the lady?
What was her answer?

16

Nasreddin had a shed behind his house. It had no lights in it. One night he went out to the shed to get his ladder, and lost his ring there. He left the ladder, went out into the street and began to look around.

One of his friends saw him in the street outside his house, and said to him, 'Hullo, Nasreddin. What are you looking for?'

'My ring,' answered Nasreddin. 'It fell off my finger. It is a silver ring with a red stone in it.'

'Oh, yes,' said his friend. 'I remember it. I will help you to look for it. Where did you lose it?'

'In my shed.'

'But why don't you look for it there?'

'Don't be stupid! It is quite dark in my shed, so how will I find my ring there? Here there is light from the lamps in the street.'

What did Nasreddin have behind his house?	Who saw him in the street?
	What did this person say?
What was his shed like?	What was Nasreddin's answer?
What did he do one night?	What did his friend say then?
Why did he do this?	What did Nasreddin answer?
What happened?	What did his friend say now?
What did Nasreddin do then?	What did Nasreddin say to him?

17

Mrs Andrews had a young cat, and it was the cat's first winter. One evening it was outside when it began to snow heavily. Mrs Andrews looked everywhere and shouted its name, but she did not find it, so she telephoned the police and said, 'I have lost a small black cat. Has anybody found one?'

'No, madam,' said the policeman at the other end. 'But cats are really very strong animals. They sometimes live for days in the snow, and when it melts or somebody finds them, they are quite all right.'

Mrs Andrews felt happier when she heard this. 'And', she said, 'our cat is very clever. She almost talks.'

The policeman was getting rather tired. 'Well then,' he said, 'why don't you put your telephone down? Perhaps she is trying to telephone you now.'

What had Mrs Andrews got?
Was it the cat's first, second, or third winter?
What happened one evening?
Where was the cat when this happened?
What did Mrs Andrews do?
Did she find the cat?
What did she do then?
What did she say?

What was the policeman's answer?
How did Mrs Andrews feel after that?
What did she say?
How was the policeman feeling now?
What did he say to Mrs Andrews?

18

One morning Nasreddin left his house with six donkeys to go to the market. After a time, he got tired and got on to one of them. He counted the donkeys, and there were only five, so he got off and went to look for the sixth. He looked and looked but did not find it, so he went back to the donkeys and counted them again. This time there were six, so he got on to one of them again and they all started.

After a few minutes he counted the donkeys again, and again there were only five! While he was counting again a friend of his passed, and Nasreddin said to him, 'I left my house with six donkeys; then I had five; then I had six again; and now I have only five! Look! One, two, three, four, five.'

'But, Nasreddin,' said his friend, 'You are sitting on a donkey too! That is the sixth! And you are the seventh!'

What did Nasreddin do one morning?
How many donkeys did he have with him?
What happened after a time?
What did Nasreddin do then?
How many donkeys did he count?
What did he do then?
Did he find the donkey?
What did he do then?

How many donkeys were there this time?
What happened then?
What did Nasreddin do after a few minutes?
How many donkeys did he count this time?
Who passed just then?
What did Nasreddin say to him?
What did his friend answer?

19

One of Nasreddin's friends loved money very much, and never gave anything to anybody. Soon he became rich.

One day, he was walking near the river with his friends when he slipped and fell in. His friends ran to help him and one of them knelt on the ground, held out his hand and said, 'Give me your hand, and I will pull you out!' The rich man's head went under the water and then came up again, but he did not give his friend his hand. Again another of his friends tried, but again the same thing happened.

Then Nasreddin said, 'Take my hand and I will pull you out!' The rich man took his hand, and Nasreddin pulled him out of the water.

'You don't know our friend very well,' he said to the others. 'When you say "Give" to him, he does nothing; but when you say "Take", he takes!'

What was Nasreddin's friend like?
What happened to him soon?
What happened one day?
What was Nasreddin's friend doing when this happened?
What did the rich man's friends do?

What did one of them do?
What did he say?
What happened then?
What did another friend do?
What happened?
What did Nasreddin say then?
What did the rich man do?
What did Nasreddin do?
What did he say?

20

One day Nasreddin bought a donkey in the market; but while he was taking it home, two thieves followed him. One of them took the rope from the donkey's neck and tied it round his friend's neck. Then he went away with the donkey.

When Nasreddin got home, he turned and saw the young man. He was very surprised. 'Where is my donkey?' he said angrily.

'I am very sorry,' said the thief, 'but once I said some very bad things to my mother, and she changed me into a donkey. But because a good man bought me, I am now a man again! Thank you!'

Nasreddin untied the man and said, 'Go! And never say bad things to your mother again!'

The next day, Nasreddin saw the same donkey in the market again! The other thief was selling it.

Nasreddin went to it and said into its ear, 'Young man, some people will never learn!'

What did Nasreddin do one day?
Who followed him?
When did they do this?
What did one of the men do?
What did he do then?
What did Nasreddin do when he got home?
How did he feel?
What did he say?

How did he say this?
What did the thief answer?
What did Nasreddin do then?
What did he say?
What happened the next day?
Why was the donkey in the market?
What did Nasreddin do then?
What did he say?

21

Nasreddin wanted to buy some new clothes, so he went to a shop. First he asked for some trousers and put them on, but then he took them off and gave them back to the shopkeeper and said, 'No, give me a coat instead of these.'

The man gave him a coat, and said, 'This one costs the same as the trousers.' Nasreddin took the coat and walked out of the shop with it. The shopkeeper ran after him and said, 'You have not paid for that coat!'

'But I gave you the trousers for the coat,' said Nasreddin. 'They cost the same as the coat, didn't they?'

'Yes,' said the shopkeeper, 'But you didn't pay for the trousers either!'

'Of course I didn't!' answered Nasreddin. 'I did not take them. I am not stupid! Nobody gives things back and then pays for them!'

What did Nasreddin want
  to do?
Where did he go?
What did he do there first?
What did he do then?
What did he say?
What did the shopkeeper do?

What did he say?
What did Nasreddin do then?
What did the shopkeeper do?
What did he say?
What was Nasreddin's answer?
What did the shopkeeper say?
What did Nasreddin say then?

22

One day, the boys of Nasreddin's village said to him, 'You have a nice, fat sheep. Will you invite us to a party to eat it with you?'

Nasreddin did not want the boys to eat his sheep, so he said, 'It is not fat enough yet.'

'But have you not heard?' they said. 'The world is going to end tomorrow, so the sheep will never get fat!'

Nasreddin was getting tired of this, so he said, 'All right, boys, we will have a picnic tomorrow, and eat the sheep.'

So the next morning they all went to the river, the boys took off their clothes and jumped into the water, and Nasreddin killed the sheep.

When the boys came out, their clothes were not there.

'Where are our clothes, Nasreddin?' they asked.

'Oh,' he answered, 'I made the fire to cook the sheep with your clothes. You will not need them again. The world is going to end today, don't you remember?'

What did the boys of
  Nasreddin's village say to
  him?
What did Nasreddin not want?
What did he say to the boys?
What did they answer?
How did Nasreddin feel
  about this?

What did he say?
What happened the next
  morning?
What did the boys do?
What did Nasreddin do?
What happened when the boys
  came out of the water?
What did they say?
What did Nasreddin answer?

23

Whenever it rained, water came through Nasreddin's roof, so one day he got his ladder, climbed up on to the roof and began to mend it. It was quite difficult and dangerous work.

While he was up there, he suddenly saw an old man in the street. This man was waving to him. He wanted Nasreddin to come down. Nasreddin thought, 'What has happened? What news has this man got for me?' So he climbed down the ladder quickly. Several times he slipped and nearly broke his neck. When he got to the bottom, the old man said, 'I am a poor man. Please give me some money.'

Nasreddin was very angry, but he said, 'Come up.' He helped the old man to climb up the ladder and on to the roof. Then he said to him, 'I am a poor man too. I have no money for you. And now go down alone. I will not help you.'

What happened whenever it rained?

What did Nasreddin do?

What was this work like?

Whom did he see in the street?

When did he see this person?

What did Nasreddin think?

What did he do?

What happened while he was doing this?

What did the old man say when Nasreddin got to the bottom?

How did Nasreddin feel?

What did he say?

What did he do?

What did he say when they were on the roof?

24

One day Mr Robinson saw a lady in the street with ten children. He was very surprised because all the children were wearing the same clothes—white caps, dark blue coats and grey trousers.

'Are all those children yours?' he asked the mother.

'Yes, they are,' she answered.

'Do you always dress them in the same clothes?' asked Mr Robinson.

'Yes,' answered the mother. 'When we had only four children, we dressed them in the same clothes because we did not want to lose any of them. It was easy to see our children when they were among other children, because they were all wearing the same clothes. And now, when we have ten, we dress them like this because we do not want to take other children home too by mistake. When there are other children among ours, it is easy to see them, because their clothes are different.'

What did Mr Robinson see one morning?
Where did he see this?
How did he feel about it?
Why did he feel like this?
What did he say?
What did the lady answer?

What did Mr Robinson say then?
What was the lady's answer?
Why did she dress her children like that when she had four?
Why did she dress them like that when she had ten?

25

Mr and Mrs Brown lived in a small house near London with their child. Sometimes Mr Brown came back from work very late, when his wife and the child were asleep, and then he opened the front door of his house with his key and came in very quietly.

But one night when he was coming home late, he lost his key, so when he reached his house, he rang the bell. Nothing happened. He rang it again. Again nothing happened—nobody moved inside the house. Mr Brown knocked at the bedroom window, he spoke to his wife, he shouted, but she did not wake up. At last he stopped and thought for a few seconds. Then he began to speak like a small child. 'Mother!' he said, 'I want to go to the lavatory!' He spoke quite quietly but at once Mrs Brown woke up. Then he spoke to her, and she opened the door for him.

Where did Mr and Mrs Brown live?

How many children did they have?

How old is the child?

What happened sometimes?

What were his wife and child doing when this happened?

What did Mr Brown do then?

How did he come in?

What happened one night?

When did this happen?

What did Mr Brown do when he reached his house?

What happened?

What did Mr Brown do then?

What happened this time?

What did Mr Brown do then?

What did his wife do?

What did Mr Brown do then?

How did Mr Brown wake his wife?

What did he do then?

What did she do?

26

Peter's uncle lived in the country. Once Peter went to stay with him for a few weeks. Whenever they went for a walk or for a drive in the car and they passed somebody, his uncle waved. Peter was surprised, and said, 'Uncle George, you know everybody here. Where did you meet them all?'

'I don't know all these people,' said his uncle.

'Then why do you wave to them?' asked Peter.

'Well, Peter,' answered his uncle, 'when I wave to some one and he knows me, he is pleased. He continues his journey with a happier heart. But when I wave to someone and he doesn't know me, he is surprised and says to himself, "Who is that man? Why did he wave to me?" So he has something to think about during the rest of his journey, and that makes his journey seem shorter. So I make everybody happy.'

Where did Peter's uncle live?   What did he say?
What did Peter once do?   What did his uncle answer?
What happened?   What did Peter ask him then?
What did Peter feel about   What was his uncle's answer?
  this?

27

It was a beautiful spring morning. There wasn't a cloud in
the sky, and the sun was warm but not too hot, so Mr Andrews
was surprised when he saw an old gentleman at the bus-stop
with a big, strong black umbrella in his hand.

Mr Andrews said to him, 'Are we going to have rain today,
do you think?'

'No', said the old gentleman, 'I don't think so.'

'Then are you carrying the umbrella to keep the sun off
you?'

'No, the sun is not very hot in spring.'

Mr Andrews looked at the big umbrella again, and the
gentleman said, 'I am an old man, and my legs are not very
strong, so I really need a walking-stick. But when I carry a
walking-stick, people say, "Look at that poor old man", and
I don't like that. When I carry an umbrella in fine weather,
people only say, "Look at that stupid man".'

What was the weather like?	What did Mr Andrews say then?
What did Mr Andrews see?	
How did he feel about this?	What was the old gentleman's answer?
Why did he feel like this?	
What did Mr Andrews say?	What did Mr Andrews do then?
What did the old gentleman answer?	What did the old gentleman say?

28

Many years ago, an English family were living in China. One evening an important Chinese officer came to visit them. It got later and later, and he still did not go, so his hostess invited him to have dinner with them. But she had very little food in the house, so she quickly went to the kitchen and spoke to her Chinese cook. He said, 'It is all right. You will have a very good dinner.'

When they all sat down to eat, the lady was very surprised, because there was a lot of very good food on the table.

After the dinner, the hostess ran to the kitchen and said to the cook, 'How did you make such a good meal in half an hour?'

'I did not make it, madam,' he said. 'I sent one of the servants to the Chinese officer's house, and he brought back the Chinese officer's dinner.'

When did this story happen?
Where were the English family living?
What happened one evening?
What did the hostess do?
Why did she do this?
Why did she go to the kitchen?
What did the cook say?

What did the English family and the Chinese officer do then?
How did the lady feel?
Why did she feel like this?
What did she do after the dinner?
What did she say to the cook?
What was his answer?

29

One day Nasreddin went to a big dinner party. He was wearing old clothes, and when he came in, nobody looked at him and nobody gave him a seat at a table. So Nasreddin went home, put on his best clothes, and then went back to the party. The host at once got up and came to meet him. He took him to the best table, gave him a good seat, and offered him the best dishes.

Nasreddin put his coat in the food and said, 'Eat, coat!'

The other guests were very surprised and said, 'What are you doing?'

Nasreddin answered, 'I was inviting my coat to eat. When I was wearing my old clothes, nobody looked at me or offered me food or drink. Then I went home and came back in these clothes, and you gave me the best food and drink. So you gave me these things for my clothes, not for myself.'

What did Nasreddin do one day?

What was he wearing?

What happened when he came in?

What did Nasreddin do then?

What happened when he went back to the party?

What did Nasreddin do then?

What did he say?

How did the other guests feel?

What did they say?

What was Nasreddin's answer?

30

Nasreddin wanted a big pot for a party, so he borrowed one from a neighbour. After the party he took it back with another small pot inside.

'Your pot had a baby while it was with us,' he said.

Of course, the neighbour was very pleased, and when Nasreddin came to borrow the big pot again for another party, he lent it to him very gladly.

This time Nasreddin did not bring the pot back, so after a few days the man went to Nasreddin's house.

'What has happened to my big pot?' he asked. 'Why have you not brought it back yet?'

'Oh, the big pot?' said Nasreddin. 'It died while it was with us.'

'Died?' said the neighbour angrily. 'But pots do not die!'

'Why do you say that?' answered Nasreddin. 'When I said, "The pot has had a baby", you did not say, "Pots do not have babies", did you?'

What did Nasreddin want?
What did he want it for?
What did he do?
What did he do after the party?
What did he say?
How did his neighbour feel?
What did Nasreddin do after that in the story?
What did his neighbour do?

What happened to the pot this time?
What did the neighbour do then?
What did he say to Nasreddin?
What was Nasreddin's answer?
What did the neighbour say then?
How did he say it?
What did Nasreddin answer?

31

One day Nasreddin's donkey was ill, so he borrowed a horse from an officer. It was a big, strong animal, and usually nobody rode it except the officer. It tried to throw Nasreddin off, but he stayed on it. Then it suddenly began to run away with him. He tried to turn it towards his house, and he tried to stop it, but it continued to run the opposite way.

One of Nasreddin's friends was working in his field and saw him riding very fast towards this friend's house. He thought, 'Why is Nasreddin riding so fast? Perhaps he has some bad news. Perhaps he is riding to my house to give me some bad news!'

He was frightened and shouted to Nasreddin, 'Nasreddin! Nasreddin! What is the matter? Where are you going?'

'I don't know!' Nasreddin shouted back. 'This stupid animal hasn't told me!'

What was the matter with
  Nasreddin's donkey one
  day?
What did he do?
What was the horse like?
Who usually rode it?
What did it try to do?
What did Nasreddin do?
What did the horse do then?

What did Nasreddin do?
What did the horse do?
Who saw Nasreddin?
What was this person doing?
What did he think?
How did he feel?
What did he shout?
What did Nasreddin shout
  back?

32

Every Saturday, Nasreddin went to the market to buy food
and other things. He put them in a big basket, but he was
old and weak, so he always paid another man to carry the
basket home for him. But one Saturday, while he was walking
home in front of the man with the basket, the man ran away
with it.

The next Saturday, when Nasreddin went to the market
again, a friend of his said, 'Look, there he is! That man stole
your things last week!'

Nasreddin at once hid behind a shop, and stayed there
until the man left the market.

His friend was very surprised. 'Why did you do that?' he
asked.

'Well,' said Nasreddin, 'that man was carrying my basket
when he left me a week ago. He will want me to pay him for
seven days' work, and that will cost me more than a basket
full of things!'

What did Nasreddin do every Saturday?	What did Nasreddin do the next Saturday?
Why did he do this?	What did a friend of his say?
What did he do with the things?	What did Nasreddin do?
What did he do then?	When did he come out?
Why did he do this?	How did his friend feel about this?
What happened one Saturday?	What did he say?
What was Nasreddin doing when this happened?	What was Nasreddin's answer?

33

Once, when Nasreddin was a boy, his mother went out for a picnic. Before she went, she said to him, 'Nasreddin, while I am away, stay near the door, and watch it all the time.' She said this because there were a lot of thieves in their town.

Nasreddin sat down beside the door. After an hour one of his uncles came. He said to Nasreddin, 'Where is your mother?'

'At a picnic,' he answered.

'Well,' said the uncle, 'we are going to visit your house this evening. Go and tell her!'

His uncle then went away, and Nasreddin began to think. 'Mother said, "Watch the door all the time!" and Uncle said, "Go and tell her"!'

He thought and thought, then at last, he pulled the door down, put it on his back and went to his mother with it!

When did this story happen?
What did Nasreddin's mother do?
What did she say to him?
When did she say it?
Why did she say this?
What did Nasreddin do?

What happened after an hour?
What did Nasreddin's uncle say?
What did Nasreddin answer?
What did his uncle say then?
What did Nasreddin do then?
What did he think?
What did he do at last?

34

Nasreddin was sitting by a window in his house one day in the middle of winter, when he heard women outside crying. He put his head out of the window, and saw a lot of people coming towards his house. They were carrying a dead man, and the women were crying, 'Oh, why are you leaving us to go to a place without light and without a fire and without food? It will be dark there, and you will be cold and hungry. Nobody will look after you, nobody will be kind to you, and nobody will love you there!'

'My God!' said Nasreddin to his wife. 'They are talking about our house. They are bringing the dead man here! Quick, lock the door! Don't let him in!'

What was Nasreddin doing at the beginning of this story?
When was this?
What did he hear?
What did he do then?
What did he see?

What were the people doing?
What were the women doing?
What were they saying?
What did Nasreddin say?
Whom did he say this to?

35

One day when Nasreddin was travelling, he came to a village. The people there said to him, 'We have had no rain for three months, and we have no water. Our corn is dying. Please help us! Pray for rain!'

Nasreddin wanted to help these poor people, so he asked for a bucket of water. There was very little water in the village, but each family gave a little, and they filled a bucket and gave it to Nasreddin.

Then Nasreddin took off his shirt and began to wash it. The people were surprised and angry. 'That water was for our children to drink, and you are washing your shirt in it!'

But Nasreddin said, 'Wait!' He hung the shirt up to dry, and at once it began to rain.

'I have only one shirt,' he said to the surprised people, 'and when I wash it and hang it up to dry, it always rains.'

What was Nasreddin doing at the beginning of this story?
What happened one day?
Who spoke to him?
What did they say?
What did Nasreddin want to do?
What did he ask for?
What did the people do?
Was this easy for them?
Why?
What did Nasreddin do then?
How did the people feel?
What did they say?
What did Nasreddin answer?
What happened then?
How did the people feel?
What did Nasreddin say to them?

36

Three people were walking along a street, first a big man, then a pretty woman, and then an old gentleman. The first two went round a corner. Suddenly the gentleman saw a piece of paper on the ground. He picked it up. It was five pounds. A few seconds later, the young woman came back. She was crying. 'I have dropped five pounds,' she said.

'Don't cry', said the gentleman. 'Here it is.' The young woman thanked him and went away. After a few seconds, the big man came back. He was looking for something. Suddenly a window opened and a small man looked out. 'I saw five pounds fall from your pocket,' he said, 'but that man gave it to a young woman.' The big man was very angry. The gentleman was frightened and gave him another five pounds. When he had gone, the young woman came back to get her one pound sixty-seven pence, and the small man came out to get his.

What people were walking along the street at the beginning of this story?

What did the first two do?

What happened then?

What did the old gentleman do?

What was the piece of paper?

What happened then?

What was the young woman doing?

What did she say?

What did the old gentleman say?

What did the young woman do?

What happened then?

What was the big man doing?

What happened after that?

What did the man at the window say?

How did the big man feel?

How did the old gentleman feel?

What did he do?

What happened when the old gentleman went away?

How much did the young woman get?

What were these three people?

37

Nasreddin liked fish very much, and when he had enough money, he bought some for his dinner when he went to the market, and took it home. But when his wife saw the fish, she always said to herself, 'Good! Now I will invite my friends to lunch and we will eat this fish. They like fish very much.'

So when Nasreddin came home in the evening after his work, the fish was never there, and his wife always said, 'Oh, your cat ate it! She is a very bad animal!' And she gave Nasreddin soup and rice for his dinner.

But one evening when this happened, Nasreddin became very angry. He took the cat and his wife to the shop near his house and weighed the cat carefully. Then he turned to his wife and said, 'My fish weighed two kilos. This cat weighs two kilos too. My fish is here, you say. Then where is my cat?'

What did Nasreddin like very much?

When did he buy some of this?

What did he buy it for?

What did he do with it then?

What did his wife say to herself when she saw it?

What happened when Nasreddin came home?

What did his wife always say?

What did she give Nasreddin for his dinner?

How did Nasreddin feel one evening when this happened?

What did he do?

What did he say to his wife then?

38

One day when Nasreddin was having a bath, he began to sing. The bathroom was small and had a stone floor, so his song was very beautiful, he thought.

'Oh,' he said, 'I sing very well. I will sing to other people too, and perhaps I will become a famous singer, and everybody in the world will want to hear me.'

So after his bath Nasreddin went up on to the flat roof of the house and began to sing his song very loudly. But he did not like it very much when he sang it there.

A man was walking across the square in front of the house, and when he heard Nasreddin, he said, 'What are you doing? You are making a terrible noise. Nobody wants to hear it.'

'Oh, you think so, do you?' answered Nasreddin. 'Well, I really sing very beautifully. Come to my bathroom and you will hear me.'

When did Nasreddin begin to sing?
What was the bathroom like?
How did the song seem to Nasreddin?
What did he say?
What did Nasreddin do after his bath?

What did he think of his song now?
Who spoke to Nasreddin?
What was this person doing?
What did he say to Nasreddin?
What did Nasreddin answer?

39

The police in the big city were looking for a thief. At last they caught him. But while they were taking photographs of him —from the front, from the left, from the right, with a hat, without a hat—he suddenly attacked the policemen and ran off. They tried to catch him, but he got away.

Then a week later the telephone rang in the police-station, and somebody said, 'You are looking for Bill Cross, aren't you?'

'Yes.'

'Well, he left here for Waterbridge an hour ago.'

Waterbridge was a small town 150 kilometres from the city. The city police at once sent four different photographs of the thief to the police in Waterbridge.

Less than twelve hours later they got a telephone call from the police in Waterbridge. 'We have caught three of the men,' they said happily, 'and we will catch the fourth this evening, we think'.

Where were the police?
What were they doing?
What happened at last?
What did the man do?
When did he do this?
What did the police do?
What happened?
What happened a week later?
What did someone say over the telephone?

What did the police answer?
What did the man say then?
Where and what was Waterbridge?
What did the city police do?
What happened less than twelve hours later?
What did the police in Waterbridge say?

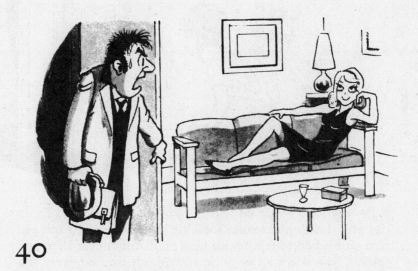

40

Mrs Jones was still cleaning the house when her husband came back from work. She was wearing dirty, old clothes and no stockings, her hair was not tidy, she had dust on her face, and she looked dirty and tired. Her husband looked at her and said, 'Is this what I come home to after a hard day's work?'

Mrs Jones's neighbour, Mrs Smith, was there. When she heard Mr Jones's words, she quickly said goodbye and ran back to her house. Then she washed, brushed and combed her hair carefully, put on her best dress and her prettiest stockings, painted her face, and waited for her husband to come home.

When he arrived, he was hot and tired. He walked slowly into the house, saw his wife and stopped. Then he shouted angrily, 'And where are *you* going this evening?'

What was Mrs Jones doing?	Who was there too?
What happened while she was doing this?	What did Mrs Smith do when she heard Mr Jones's words?
What was Mrs Jones wearing?	How was her husband when he arrived?
What did her hair look like?	
What did her face look like?	What did he do?
What did Mrs Jones look like?	What did he shout?
What did her husband say?	How did he shout this?

41

Billy was four years old and he was a very bad boy. Every day after lunch his mother took him to his bedroom and put him on his bed to rest for an hour, but Billy never slept and usually he made a lot of noise and got off his bed every few minutes.

One afternoon, Billy's mother put him on his bed and then went to her bedroom to do some sewing. After ten minutes, she heard a noise so she went to Billy's room. He was not there, but his trousers were lying on his bed.

She looked in the other rooms upstairs, but he was not there either, so she went to the top of the stairs and shouted down angrily, 'Are you running about down there without your trousers?'

'No, madam,' answered a man's voice. 'I have brought your vegetables—and I am *wearing* my trousers.'

How old was Billy?
What kind of boy was he?
What happened every day?
When did it happen?
Why did Billy's mother put him on his bed?
What did Billy do then?
What happened one afternoon?
Why did Billy's mother go to her bedroom?
What happened after ten minutes?

What did Billy's mother do then?
What did she see in Billy's room?
What did she do then?
What did she see?
What did she do after that?
What did she shout?
How did she shout this?
Who answered?
What did he say?

42

An old lady in an aeroplane had a blanket over her head and she did not want to take it off. The air hostess spoke to her, but the old lady said, 'I have never been in an aeroplane before, and I am frightened. I am going to keep this blanket over my head until we are back on the ground again!'

Then the captain came. He said 'Madam, I am the captain of this aeroplane. The weather is fine, there are no clouds in the sky, and everything is going very well.' But she continued to hide.

So the captain turned and started to go back. Then the old lady looked out from under the blanket with one eye and said, 'I am sorry, young man, but I don't like aeroplanes and I am never going to fly again. But I'll say one thing,' she continued kindly, 'you and your wife keep your aeroplane very clean!'

Where was the old lady?	What did this person say?
What was she doing at the beginning of this story?	What did the old lady do?
Who spoke to her?	What did the captain do?
What did the old lady say?	What did the old lady do then?
Who came then?	What did she say?

43

A young air force officer had a very beautiful wife. Early each morning he left his house and went to the airport, and an hour later his wife always left the house too, with a big white towel, and went for a walk on the beach.

Her husband always flew over every morning, and when she saw his aeroplane, she held the white towel high above her head. When her husband saw it, he made either the left wing or the right wing of his aeroplane go down. The left wing meant, 'I will be busy tonight and won't be home.' The right wing meant, 'In eight hours I will be holding you in my arms.'

One morning he flew over with eight other aeroplanes, and his left wing went down. Before his wife had time to feel sad about this, all the other aeroplanes flew over, and each of them turned its right wing down.

Who are the two people at the beginning of this story?

When did the man in this story leave his house?

Where did he go?

When did his wife leave the house?

What did she take with her?

Where did she go?

What happened every morning after that?

What did the officer's wife do?

When did she do it?

What did her husband do then?

When did he do this?

What did the left wing mean?

What did the right wing mean?

What happened one morning?

Which wing went down?

What did the other aeroplanes do?

44

An artist had a small daughter. Sometimes he painted women without any clothes on, and he and his wife always tried to keep the small girl out when he was doing this. 'She is too young to understand,' they said.

But one day, when the artist was painting a woman with no clothes on, he forgot to lock the door, and the little girl suddenly ran into the room. Her mother ran up the stairs after her, but when she got to the top, the little girl was already in the room and looking at the woman. Both her parents waited for her to speak.

For a few seconds the little girl said nothing, but then she ran to her mother and said angrily, 'Why do you let her go about without shoes and socks on when you don't let me?'

What was the small girl's father?

What did he sometimes do?

What did he and his wife do then?

What did they say?

What happened one day?

When did it happen?

What did the small girl's mother do?

What was the girl doing when her mother got to the top of the stairs?

What did her parents do?

What did the little girl do?

What did she say?

How did she feel about this?

45

It was a small factory, and there was nowhere to eat near it, so the workmen took food from their homes and ate it in the factory at midday.

One of the workmen always had fish sandwiches. Every day he took one of them out of his bag, bit it, and then threw all the sandwiches angrily away.

At last, one day one of the workmen said to him, 'But, Bill, don't you like fish sandwiches?'

'No,' said Bill, 'I hate them.'

'Then why does your wife make them for you every day? There are lots of other nice things for sandwiches. Tell your wife, and she will make other sandwiches.'

'It isn't as easy as that,' answered Bill. 'I haven't got a wife. I make the sandwiches myself.'

Where did the workmen in the story work?

What did they take to the factory?

Why did they do this?

When and where did they eat their food?

What did one of the workmen always have?

What did he do every day?

How did he feel?

What did another workman say to him one day?

What did Bill answer?

What did the other workman say then?

What was Bill's answer to this?

46

Mrs Brown had a small garden behind her house, and in the spring she planted some vegetables in it. She looked after them very carefully, and when the summer came, they looked very nice.

One evening Mrs Brown looked at her vegetables and said, 'Tomorrow I am going to pick them, and then we can eat them.'

But early the next morning, her son ran into the kitchen and shouted, 'Mother, Mother! Come quickly! Our neighbour's ducks are in the garden and they are eating our vegetables!'

Mrs Brown ran out, but it was too late! All the vegetables were finished! Mrs Brown cried, and her neighbour was very sorry, but that was the end of the vegetables.

Then a few days before Christmas, the neighbour brought Mrs Brown a parcel. In it was a beautiful, fat duck, and on it was a piece of paper with the words, 'Enjoy your vegetables!'

What did Mrs Brown have?
Where did she have it?
What did she do there?
When did she do it?
What did she do then?
What happened in the summer?
What did Mrs Brown do one evening?
What did she say?
What happened early the next morning?

What did Mrs Brown's son shout?
What did Mrs Brown do?
What happened to the vegetables?
How did Mrs Brown's neighbour feel?
What happened a few days before Christmas?
What was in the parcel?
What were the words on the piece of paper?

47

The ladies' club always had a meeting every Friday afternoon and someone came to talk to them about important things. After that, they had tea and asked questions.

One Friday, a gentleman came and talked to the club about food. 'There is not enough food in the world for everybody,' he said. 'More than half the people in the world are hungry. And when they get more food, they have more babies, so they never stop being hungry. Somewhere in the world, a woman is having a baby every minute, day and night. What are *we* going to do about it?' He waited for a few seconds before he continued, but before he began to speak again, one of the ladies said, 'Well, why don't we find that woman and *stop* her?'

What happened every Friday afternoon?

What happened at the meeting?

What happened after that?

What happened one Friday?

What did the man say?

What question did he ask?

What did he do then?

What did one of the ladies say?

48

A man had some work to do in Switzerland, so he said good-bye to his wife at the airport, got into an aeroplane and left. After ten days, his work in Switzerland was finished, so he bought a ticket for his journey back home, and then went to the post-office to send a telegram to his wife. He wrote the telegram, gave it to the clerk and said, 'How much will this cost?'

She told him, and he counted his Swiss money. He had not got quite enough.

'Take the word "love" off my telegram,' he said, 'and then I will have enough money to pay for it.'

'No,' the girl said. She opened her handbag, took the money for the word 'love' out of it and said, 'For the word "love", I will pay the money. Wives need that word from their husbands.'

Why did the man in this story go to Switzerland?

What did he do at the airport?

What happened after ten days?

What did he do then?

Why did he go to the post-office?

What did he do there?

What did he say to the clerk?

What did she do?

What did the man do then?

Had he got enough money?

What did he say then?

What did the girl say?

What did she do?

What did she say then?

49

Mrs Jones's telephone number was 3463, and the number of the cinema in her town was 3464, so people often made a mistake and telephoned her when they wanted the cinema.

One evening the telephone bell rang and Mrs Jones answered it. A tired man said, 'At what time does your last film begin?'

'I am sorry,' said Mrs Jones, 'but you have the wrong number. This is not the cinema.'

'Oh, it began twenty minutes ago?' said the man. 'I am sorry about that. Goodbye.'

Mrs Jones was very surprised, so she told her husband. He laughed and said, 'The man's wife wanted to go to the cinema, but he was feeling tired, so he telephoned the cinema. His wife heard *him*, but she didn't hear *you*. Now they will stay at home this evening, and the husband will be happy!'

What did people often do in this story?
Why did they do this?
What happened one evening?
What did Mrs Jones do?
Who spoke to her on the telephone?

What did he say?
What did Mrs Jones answer?
What did the man say then?
How did Mrs Jones feel?
What did she do?
What did her husband do?
What did he say?

50

It was a few days before Christmas, so when the office closed at half past five, most of the young men and typists stayed and had a party. They ate and drank, danced and sang songs, and nobody wanted to go home. But Joe had a wife at home, and lived quite a long way from the city. Every few minutes he looked at his watch, and at last, when it was very late, he began to leave.

'Joe!' shouted his friends. 'Are you leaving? Why don't you stay and enjoy the party?'

'I am not leaving,' said Joe. 'I am only going down to the station to miss the last train back home. I will be back here in a few minutes.'

When did this story happen?	What did he have at home?
What happened at half past five?	What did he do every few minutes?
What happened after that?	What did he do at last?
What did the people do?	When did he do this?
What did they not want to do?	What did his friends shout?
Where did Joe live?	What was Joe's answer?

5 1

Mr Jones and Mr Brown worked in the same office. One day Mr Jones said to Mr Brown, 'We are going to have a small party at our house next Wednesday evening. Will you and your wife come?'

Mr Brown said, 'Thank you very much. That is very kind of you. We are free that evening, I think, but I will telephone my wife and ask her. Perhaps she wants to go somewhere that evening.' So Mr Brown went to the other room and telephoned. When he came back, he looked very surprised.

'What is the matter?' said Mr Jones. 'Did you speak to your wife?'

'No,' answered Mr Brown. 'She wasn't there. My small son answered the telephone. I said to him, "Is your mother there, David?" and he answered, "No, she is not in the house". "Where is she then?" I asked. "She is somewhere outside". "What is she doing?" "She is looking for me".

Where did Mr Jones and
  Mr Brown work?
What did Mr Jones say to
  Mr Brown one day?
What did Mr Brown answer?

What did he do then?
How did he look when he came
  back?
What did Mr Jones say to him?
What was Mr Brown's answer?

52

When you have a post-office box, the postman does not bring letters to you, but *you* go to the post-office and get your letters and parcels from your box. The box is locked, and you have the key, so the letters are quite safe.

One day, the headmaster of a school wrote to the post-office and asked for a post-office box for his school. He soon got an answer. It said, 'We will give you a post-box in one month.'

Three months later, the headmaster wrote to the post-office again and said, 'Why haven't we got a post-office box yet?'

This was the answer from the post-office:

'Dear Sir,

We gave you a post-office box two months ago and wrote to you then to tell you. Here is the key to your box. You will find our letter to you in it.'

What happens when you have a post-office box?

Why are the letters safe when they are in a post-office box?

What happened one day?

What happened then?

What was the answer?

What happened three months later?

What was the answer from the post-office?

53

One night there was a heavy snowstorm, and in the morning Mr Smith's garden was full of deep snow. Mr Smith wanted to take his car out, so he paid a man to clean the path from his garage to his gate. He said to this man, 'Don't throw any snow on that side, because it will damage the bushes in my garden; and don't throw any on the other side, because it will break my fence. And don't throw any into the street, or the police will be angry.' Then Mr Smith went out.

When he came back, the path was clean and the snow from it was not on the bushes, or the fence, or the street. Mr Smith was very pleased—until he opened the garage to get his car out! The garage was full to the top with all the snow from the path, and his car was somewhere under it all!

What happened one night?
What was Mr Smith's garden like in the morning?
What did he do then?
Why did he do this?
What did he say to the man?
What did he do then?

What did he see when he came back?
How did he feel?
For how long did he feel like this?
What was the garage like?
Where was the car?

54

At the beginning of the First World War, John Robinson was a soldier in the army. He went to France with a lot of other soldiers, and lived in a cold, wet, muddy camp. The rain came into his tent, there was mud and water on the floor, and the food was not good.

Then he became an officer and went to work in the army in Paris. He lived very pleasantly there in a warm house, had very good food, and enjoyed himself.

After some months, he met one of his old friends from the camp.

'You made a big mistake when you left our camp,' said this friend.

'Oh?' said John Robinson. 'Why?'

'Well,' said the soldier, 'the week after you left, they put wood floors in our tents!'

When did this story happen?
What was John Robinson?
Where did he go?
Whom did he go with?
Where did he live?
What was the camp like?
What was John's tent like?
How was the food at the camp?
What happened then?
Where did he go?

How did he live there?
Where did he live?
How did he like it?
What happened after some months?
What did his friend say?
What did John Robinson answer?
What did his friend say then?

55

Mr Andrews had a new telephone number. Before he got
it, it was the number of a shop. The shop now had a new
number, but a lot of women did not know this, so they still
telephoned the old one.

At first, Mr and Mrs Andrews always said, 'We are sorry.
You have the wrong number. The shop has a new one now.'

But women still continued to telephone them to ask
for things, so after some time, Mr and Mrs Andrews began
to answer them like this:

'Good morning, madam. What do you want us to send
you today?' They thought, 'Perhaps they will stop tele-
phoning us when they don't get their things . But this
did not help Mr and Mrs Andrews, because now women
began to telephone them more and more, and say angrily,
'Where are my things? They have not come yet! Why haven't
you sent them yet?'

What did Mr Andrews have?
What was it before he got it?
What happened then?
Why did it happen?
What did Mr and Mrs
  Andrews always do at first?
What happened after that?

What did Mr and Mrs Andrews
  do after some time?
Why did they do this?
Did this help Mr and Mrs
  Andrews?
Why?

56

It was Christmas, and there was a big party in the house.
Guests came and went, but the party continued. Then the
bell rang. Several people shouted, 'Come in!' and a small
man opened the front door and came in. Nobody knew him,
but the host went to meet him and took him to the bar for a
drink. The man sat there happily for an hour and a half and
drank. Then suddenly he stopped and looked at his host.
'Do you know,' he said, 'nobody invited me to this party.
I don't know you, I don't know your wife and I don't know
any of your guests. My wife and I wanted to go out in our
car, but one of your guests' cars was in front of our gate, so
I came here to find him—and my wife is waiting in our car
for me to come back!'

When did this story happen?
What was there in the house?
What did the guests do?
What happened to the party
    then?
What happened after that?
Who shouted?

What did they shout?

What happened then?
Who knew the small man?
What did the host do?
What did the small man do
    after that?
For how long did he do this?
What did he do then?

What did he say to his host?

A 1000-word Vocabulary

Note : This vocabulary does not contain numerals, names of the days of the week, names of the months or proper nouns and adjectives. Not all cases of noun and pronouns are given (e.g. *boy* stands for *boy—boy's—boys —boys'*; *I* stands for *I—me— my—mine*); nor are all parts of verbs given (e.g. *swim* stands for *swim—swims—swam—swum* *—swimming*). Comparatives and superlatives of adjectives and adverbs are also not given.

The abbreviation a. means adjective and/or adverb; n. means noun; and v. means verb.

Three words have been added to the 1000-word vocabulary — *beer*, *call* (n.) and *market*. They are given in *italic* in the following list.

a(n)	around	beard	boot
about	arrive	beat (v.)	born
above	artist	beautiful	borrow
absent (a.)	as	because	both
accept	ask	become	bottle
accident	asleep	bed	bottom
ache	at	bee	bowl (n.)
across	attack	*beer*	box (n.)
address (n.)	aunt	before	boy
aeroplane	autumn	begin(ning)	branch
afraid	avoid	behind	brave
after	awake	bell	bread
afternoon	away	belong	break
again		belt	breakfast
against	baby	bench	bridge
ago	back (a.)	besides	bright
air force	back (n.)	between	bring
air(port)	bad (worse/worst)	bicycle	broken
all	bag	big	brother
almost	bake	bill	brown
alone	ball	bird	brush
along	balloon	birthday	bucket
also	banana	bite	build(ing)
although	bandage	bitter	bunch
always	bank	black	burn
a.m.	bar	blackboard	burst
ambulance	barber	blanket	bus
among	bargain	blood	bush
and	basin	blouse	busy
angry	basket	blow	but
animal	bath	blue	butter
answer	bathe	boat	button
ant	battle	body (and -body,	buy
any	be	e.g. in *anybody*)	by
apple	beach	boil (v.)	
arm	bean	bomb	cage
army	bear (n.)	book	cake

call	come	dream	find
camera	common	dress	fine (a.)
camp	continue	drink	finger
can (n.)	cook	drive	finish(ed)
canal	cool	drop (n.)	fire
cap	copy	dry	first
captain	corn	duck	fish(erman)
car	corner	during	flag
card	correct	duster	flat (a.)
careful	cost	dust(y)	floor
careless	cotton(-wool)		flour
carpet	cough	each	flower
carriage	count (v.)	ear	fly (n.)
carry	country	early	fly (v.)
cart	course	earth	follow
cat	cover(ed)	east	food
catch	cow	easy	foot(ball)
ceiling	cross (n.)	eat	for
chain	cross (v.)	egg	foreign
chair	crowd(ed)	either	forest
chalk	cry	electric(ity)	forget
change	cup	elephant	fork
cheap	cupboard	else	forward
cheek	curtain	empty	free
cheese	cut	end	fresh
chemist	cycle (v.)	enemy	friend
chest		engine	frighten(ed)
chicken	damage(d)	enjoy	from
child	damp	enough	front
chimney	dance	equal	fruit
chin	dangerous	evening	fry
chocolate	dark	ever	full
choose	date	every(where)	funny
church	daughter	examination	furniture
cigarette	day	except	
cinema	dead	excuse	game
circle	deep	exercise	garage
city	dentist	expensive	garden
class	desk	eye	gas
clean	die		gate
clerk	different	face	gentleman
clever	difficult	factory	get
climate	dining (-room,	fall	girl
climb	-hall)	family	give
clock	dinner	famous	glad
close (v.)	dirty	far	glass
cloth	discover	farm(er)	glue
clothes	dish	fast	go
cloud(y)	dive	fat	goal
club	do	father	goat
coat	doctor	feel	God
cock	dog	fence	good (better/best)
coffee	donkey	few	goodbye
cold	door	field	gramophone
collar	double	fierce	grand- (e.g. in
collect	down	fight	*grandfather*)
colour	Dr	fill	grass
comb	draw	film	green

61

grey	I	let	Miss
grill	ice(-cream)	letter	mistake
ground	ill	lid	mix
group	important	lie (v.)	model
grow	in(to)	light (a.)	money
guest	injection	light (n. and v.)	monkey
gun	ink	like (a.)	month
	inside	like (v.)	moon
hair	instead	line	more
half	interesting	lion	morning
hall	invite	listen	mosque
hammer	iron	little	most
hand	island	live (v.)	mother
handkerchief	it	living-room	mountain
hang		loaf	mouse
happen	jam	lock(ed)	moustache
happy	jar	long (a.)	mouth
hard	joke	look	move
hat	journey	lose	Mr(s)
hate	jug	lot	much
have	jump	loud	mud(dy)
he		love	music
head	keep	lucky	
headmaster/	key	luggage	nail
mistress	kick	lump	name
hear	kill	lunch	narrow
heart	kilo(gram)		nasty
heavy	kilometre	machine	near
help	kind (a.)	madam	necessary
hen	kind (n.)	magazine	neck
here	kitchen	main	need
hide (v.)	kite	make	needle
high	kneel	man	neighbour
hill	knife	many	neither
history	knock	map	nephew
hit	know	marbles	nest
hobby		*market*	net
hold	ladder	marry	never
hole	lady	mat	new
holiday	lake	match	news(paper)
home(work)	lamp	mathematics	next
honey	land	matter	nice
hook	language	meal	niece
hooray	last	mean (v.)	night
horse	late	measure	no
hospital	laugh	meat	noise (noisy)
host(ess)	lavatory	medicine	none
hot	lay	meet(ing)	nor
hotel	lazy	melt	north
hour	leaf	mend	nose
house	learn	metre	not
how	least	midday	now
hullo	leave	middle	number
hungry	left	midnight	nurse
hurry	leg	milk	nut
hurt	lend	mind	
husband	less	minute (n.)	o'clock
	lesson	miss (v.)	of

off	please(d)	road	shorts
offer	plough	roar	shout
office	p.m.	rock	show
officer	pocket	roll	shut
often	poem	roof	shy
oh	point (v.)	room	sick
oil	poisonous	rope	side
old	police(man)	rose	silver
on	pond	rough	since
once	pool (e.g.	round	sing(er)
one (and -one,	swimming-pool)	row (v.)	sir
e.g. in anyone)	poor	rub	sister
only	port	rubber	sit
open	post (-card,	rug	size
opposite	-man, -office)	ruler	skirt
or	pot	run	sky
orange	potato		sleep(y)
other	pound	sad	slice
out	pour	safe	slide
outside	pray	sail	slip(pery)
oven	prefer	salt	slow
over	present (a.)	same	small
owe	present (n.)	sand(y)	smell
	pretty	sandwich	smile
page	price	save	smoke
pain	pull	say	smooth
paint	punctual	school	snake
paper	pupil	scissors	snow
parcel	push	score	so
parent	put	sea	soap
park		seat	sock
party	quarter	second (n.)	soft
pass	question	see	soldier
passenger	quick	seldom	some
past	quiet	-self/-selves	sometimes
path	quite	sell	son
patient (a.)		send	song
pay	race	sentence	soon
pen	radio	servant	sorry
pencil	rain(y)	several	soup
penny	rat	sew(ing)	sour
people	rather	shade (shady)	south
perhaps	reach	shake	speak
person	read	shallow	spell
petrol	ready	shape	spend
photograph	real	sharp	spill
pick	red	she	spoil
picnic	remember	shed	spoon(ful)
picture	repeat	sheep	sport
piece	rest	sheet	spring (n.)
pile	restaurant	shelf	square
pillow	rice	shine	stain
pink	rich	ship	stairs (also -stairs,
place	ride	shirt	e.g. in upstairs)
plant	right	shoe	stale
plate	ring (n.)	shoot	stamp
play(ground)	ring (v.)	shop(keeper)	stand
pleasant	river	short	star

start	thank	university	with(out)
station	that/those	until	woman
stay	the	up	wood
steal	theatre	useful	wool
steep	then	useless	word
step	there	usually	work
stick (n.)	they		world
sticky	thick	valley	write
still	thief	van	wrong
sting	thin	vegetable	
stocking	thing (also -thing	very	year
stomach	e.g. in *nothing*)	village	yellow
stone	think	visit(or)	yes
stop	thirsty	volley-ball	yesterday
storm(y)	this/these	voyage	yet
story	through		you
stove	throw	wait	young
straight	ticket	wake	
strange	tidy	walk(ing-stick)	zoo
street	tie (v.)	wall	
string	tiger	want	
strong	till	warm	
student	time	wash	
study	tin	watch (n.)	
stupid	tired	watch (v.)	
such	to	water	
suddenly	today	wave	
sugar	together	way	
sum	tomorrow	we	
summer	tongue	weak	
sun(ny)	tonight	wear	
surprised	too	weather	
sweep	tooth	week	
sweet	top	weigh	
swim(mer)	towards	well (a.)	
sword	towel	west	
	tower	wet	
table	town	what	
tail	toy	wheel	
take	train (n.)	when(ever)	
talk	travel	where (also -where	
tall	tree	e.g. in *nowhere*)	
tame	trip	which	
tank	trouble	while	
tap	trousers	white	
taste	truck	who	
tea	true	why	
teach(er)	try	wide	
team	turn	wife	
tear (v.)	twice	wild	
telegram	type (v.)	will (v.)	
telephone	typist	win	
tell		wind(y)	
temple	ugly	window	
tennis	umbrella	wing	
tent	uncle	winter	
terrible	under	wipe	
than	understand	wire	

Elementary Stories for Reproduction 2

L. A. Hill

Oxford University Press
外 國 語 研 修 社

Oxford University Press
OXFORD LONDON GLASGOW
NEW YORK TORONTO MELBOURNE AUCKLAND
KUALA LUMPUR SINGAPORE HONG KONG TOKYO
DELHI BOMBAY CALCUTTA MADRAS KARACHI
NAIROBI DAR ES SALAAM CAPE TOWN
and associates in
BEIRUT BERLIN IBADAN MEXICO CITY NICOSIA

© *Oxford University Press (Tokyo) 1977*

First published 1977
Tenth impression 1982

First Korean impression 1985
Second Korean impression 1993

ISBN 0 19 580242 X (East Asia Edition)
ISBN 0 19 581762 1 (UK Edition)

Illustrated by Dennis Mallet

Printed in Korea

Introduction

In this book there are 56 stories, each about 150 words long, which can be used for oral or written reproduction work. Here are some ways in which these stories can be used:

(i) *Listening and Speaking*

Only the teacher has the book. He reads one of the stories aloud to the students two or three times, and they have to retell the story orally, or to answer oral questions[1] about it. This is best done in very small classes, of course.

(ii) *Listening and Writing*

Only the teacher has the book. He reads one of the stories aloud to the students two or three times, and they then write down as much of it as they can remember, or answer questions about it in writing (these questions can be written on the blackboard or dictated by the teacher). This can be done in a large class.

The listening tape, which is available separately, can be used for both (i) and (ii), by the teacher in group teaching or by an individual student working on his own.

(iii) *Reading and Writing*

Each student has a copy of the book. He reads one of the stories for a certain number of minutes, then shuts the book and writes down as much of the story as he remembers, or answers questions about it in writing. The questions can be written on the blackboard or dictated by the teacher.

With (i), (ii) and (iii), there can be an interval of time—even of several days—between the telling or reading of the story and the reproduction.

(iii) can be done by students who have not got a teacher. They can read, close their books, and then write down as much of the story as they can remember. When they have finished, they can open their books again and check what they have written by referring to the story in the book.

All the stories in this book are written within the 1,000 word vocabulary of my *Elementary Comprehension Pieces* and *Elementary Composition Pieces* (both published by Oxford University Press). This vocabulary is given in the appendix to this book.

The grammatical structures used in this book are also strictly limited. For example, no conditionals, passives, relative clauses, reported speech or modal auxiliaries are used; and the tenses are limited to the present simple, the present continuous, the present perfect, the simple future with *will*, the *going to* future, the past simple and the past continuous.

[1] Suggested questions follow each piece.

(ii) gives practice in aural comprehension (listening and understanding).

In addition, the student working on his own can do (iii):

(iii) He can read the story to himself, aloud or silently, once or more than once, and then write down as much of the story as he can remember, and/or answer the questions and do the exercises, all without looking at the story again. If he writes as much of the story as he can remember he can check his work afterwards by comparing it with the story in the book.

(iii) gives practice in reading comprehension (reading and understanding).

With (ii) and (iii) there can be an interval—even of several days—between the hearing or reading of the story and the reproduction (writing down as much as one can remember).

A separate Teacher's Booklet is available, containing model answers to the exercises.

Elementary Stories for Reproduction 2

1

Jack was a young sailor. He lived in England, but he was often away with his ship.

One summer he came back from a long voyage and found new neighbours near his mother's house. They had a pretty daughter, and Jack soon loved her very much.

He said to her, 'My next voyage will begin in a few days' time, Gloria. I love you, and I'll marry you when I come back. I'll think about you all the time, and I'll write to you and send you a present from every port.'

Jack's first port was Freetown in Africa, and he sent Gloria a parrot from there. It spoke five languages.

When Jack's ship reached Australia, there was a letter from Gloria. It said, 'Thank you for the parrot, Jack. It tasted much better than a chicken.'

Words outside the 1000: parrot, sailor

A. Answer these questions.

1. Why did Jack make long voyages?
2. Where did Gloria live?
3. Why did Jack think about Gloria all the time?
4. Where did Jack send Gloria the parrot from?
5. Where did Jack get Gloria's letter about the parrot?
6. What did Gloria do to the parrot?

B. Which words in the story on page 4 mean the opposite of:

1. short   4. old   7. worse
2. last   5. little
3. ugly   6. winter

C. Write this story. Put one word in each empty place. You will find all the correct words in the story on page 4.

Freetown is a . . . in West Africa. Jack and another . . . from his ship went into a shop there and saw a beautiful bird. It was a red and grey . . . , and it . . . , 'Hullo,' to them. Jack said to his friend, 'I'm going to . . . it to Gloria. She's the daughter of my mother's . . . . It will be a nice . . . for her.' Then Jack and his friend . . . a restaurant and ate . . . and fried potatoes there. They . . . very good.

2

Fanny and Ethel worked in the same office, and they were neighbours at home. Fanny was rather a careless girl, and she often lost things. Then she usually went to Ethel to borrow more from her.

Ethel was a kind girl, but she sometimes got tired of lending things to her friend.

One Saturday afternoon Fanny knocked at Ethel's front door, and when Ethel came to open it, Fanny said to her, 'Oh, hullo, Ethel. Please lend me a bag. I've lost mine. I'm going to the shops, and I feel very stupid when I haven't got anything in my hand when I go out in the street.'

Ethel laughed and answered, 'Well, Fanny, go down to the end of the garden. You'll find a nice wheelbarrow in the shed there. Take that when you go down to the shops. Then you'll have something in *both* of your hands.'

Word outside the 1000: wheelbarrow

A. Answer these questions.

1. Why did Fanny often lose things?
2. Why did Ethel lend things to Fanny?
3. Why didn't Fanny want to go to the shops without a bag?
4. Why didn't Ethel lend her a bag?
5. What did she want Fanny to take to the shops?
6. Did Fanny take it, do you think?

B. Which of these sentences are true? Write the correct ones down.

1. Ethel often borrowed things.
2. Fanny often borrowed things.
3. Ethel often lent things to Fanny.
4. Fanny often lent things to Ethel.
5. One day Ethel lost her bag.
6. One day Fanny lost her bag.
7. Fanny liked carrying something in her hand.
8. Fanny did not like carrying things.
9. There was a shed at the end of Ethel's garden.
10. There was a shed at the end of Fanny's garden.

C. Write this story, but do not put pictures: put words.

Ethel's house is in a small . It has a small
 at the back, and there is a in it.

Ethel keeps her there. Ethel is a clever

 . She works in a big . This is

Ethel. She is at the of her house, and she has got

a in her left , because she is going

to the

73

3

Dave married, and when his new wife saw the clothes in his cupboard, she said, 'Dave, you have only got one good shirt. The others are very old, and they've got holes in them. I'm going to buy you a new one this afternoon.'

Dave liked his old shirts, but he loved his wife too, so he said, 'All right, Beryl, but please don't throw any of the old ones away.'

Dave went to work, and when he came back in the evening, Beryl said to him, 'Look, Dave, I've bought you a nice shirt. Here it is. Put it on.'

Dave put the shirt on, and then he said, 'Look at the sleeves, Beryl. They're too long.'

'That's all right,' Beryl answered. 'They'll get shorter when I wash the shirt.'

Then Dave said, 'But the neck's too small.'

'That's all right,' Beryl answered. 'It'll get bigger when you wear the shirt, Dave.'

Word outside the 1000: **sleeve**

A. Answer these questions.

1. Why did Beryl want to buy Dave a new shirt?
2. Why didn't Dave want his wife to throw any of his old shirts away?
3. Why didn't Dave like the sleeves of his new shirt?
4. What did Beryl say about the sleeves?
5. Why didn't Dave like the collar of the shirt?
6. What did Beryl say about the collar?

B. *Opposites.* **Write these sentences. Put one word in each empty place.**

1. New clothes do not have holes in them, but . . . ones sometimes do.
2. Sleeves don't get . . . when you wash them. They get shorter.
3. Good shirts are not cheap. They are . . . .
4. The neck of Dave's shirt wasn't too big. It was too . . . .
5. Dave loved his old shirts, but he . . . his new one.

C. Choose the right sentence for each picture and write it down.

1. a. None of these shirts has got holes in it.
   b. Some of these shirts have got holes in them.
   c. All of these shirts have got holes in them.

2. a. The sleeves are too long,
      and the collar is too small.
   b. The sleeves are too short,
      and the collar is too small.
   c. The sleeves are too short,
      and the collar is too big.
   d. The sleeves are too long,
      and the collar is too big.

4

Mrs. Williams lived in a small street in London, and now she had a new neighbour. Her name was Mrs. Briggs, and she talked a lot about her expensive furniture, her beautiful carpets and her new kitchen.

'Do you know,' she said to Mrs. Williams one day, 'I've got a new dishwasher. It washes the plates and glasses and knives and forks beautifully.'

'Oh?' Mrs. Williams answered. 'And does it dry them and put them in the cupboard too?'

Mrs. Briggs was surprised. 'Well,' she answered, 'the things in the machine are dry after an hour, but it doesn't put them away, of course.'

'I've had a dishwasher for twelve and a half years,' Mrs. Williams said.

'Oh?' Mrs. Briggs answered. 'And does *yours* put the things in the cupboard when it has washed them?' She laughed nastily.

'Yes, he does,' Mrs. Williams answered. 'He dries the dishes *and* puts them away.'

Word outside the 1000: dishwasher

A. Answer these questions.

1. Where did Mrs. Briggs live?
2. Why was Mrs. Briggs surprised?
3. Did Mrs. Briggs's dishwasher dry the plates and other things?
4. Did it put them away?
5. Did Mrs. Williams's dishwasher put the things in the cupboard?
6. Who was Mrs. Williams's dishwasher?

B. Write these sentences. Put one of these words in each empty place:

> *an   any   no   none   some*

1. Mrs. Briggs was rich, but Mrs. Williams was not. Mrs. Briggs had . . . beautiful carpets, but Mrs. Williams didn't have . . . .
2. Mrs. Briggs had . . . expensive furniture, but Mrs. Williams had . . . .
3. Mrs. Briggs had . . . expensive dishwasher, but Mrs. Williams did not have . . . machines in her kitchen.
4. Mrs. Briggs had . . . nice roses in her garden, but Mrs. Williams had . . . flowers in hers.
5. Mrs. Briggs had . . . big trees in her garden too, but Mrs. Williams had . . . .

C. Write this story. Put one of these words in each empty place:

> *he   him   his   her   it   its   she*

Mrs. Williams had a good baby: . . . never cried, and . . . clothes were always clean. Mrs. Briggs was very surprised and said, 'When my daughter was small, I gave . . . lots of food, but . . . cried a lot, and . . . clothes were always dirty. Why is your baby so different? How do you do . . . ?'

'Well,' answered Mrs. Williams, 'my first child was a boy. I always gave . . . a lot of food, . . . got very fat, and . . . stomach was always full. He cried a lot and was dirty. Now I give my new baby much less, and . . . is happy and clean.'

5

One day a man went to see his doctor and said to him, 'I've swallowed a horse, doctor, and I feel very ill.'

The doctor thought for a few seconds and then said, 'All right, Mr. Lloyd, I'll help you. Please lie down on this bed.'

The doctor's nurse gave the man an injection, the man went to sleep, and the doctor went out quickly to look for a horse in the town.

After half an hour he found one, borrowed it and took it into his office, so when Mr. Lloyd woke up, it was there in front of him.

'Here's the horse, Mr. Lloyd,' the doctor said. 'I've taken it out of your stomach, and it won't give you any more trouble now.'

At first Mr. Lloyd was happy, but then he looked at the horse again and said, 'But, doctor, my horse was white, and this one's brown!'

Word outside the 1000: swallowed

A. Answer these questions.

1. Did the doctor think, 'This man has really swallowed a horse'?
2. Why did the nurse give the man an injection?
3. What did the doctor do when he went out?
4. What did Mr. Lloyd see when he woke up?
5. Why was Mr. Lloyd not happy when he looked at the horse more carefully?

B. Which words in the story on page 12 mean:

1. sick   3. visit   5. discovered
2. pleased   4. fast

C. Put the number of the correct sentence under the correct picture.

  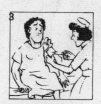

1. The nurse gave Mr. Lloyd an injection.
2. The doctor went out into the street.
3. Mr. Lloyd said, 'I feel very ill.'
4. Mr. Lloyd woke up.
5. Mr. Lloyd came into the doctor's office.
6. Mr. Lloyd went to sleep.

6

A history teacher was talking to his class about the ancient Romans.

'They were very strong, brave people, and they were good soldiers,' he said. 'They always wanted to have strong bodies, so they played a lot of games.'

'Did they like swimming?' one of the girls asked. 'That makes people's bodies strong.' She was very good at swimming.

'Oh, yes, some of them swam a lot,' the teacher answered. Then he told them a story about one famous Roman.

'There was a big, wide river in the middle of Rome,' he said. 'It was the Tiber, and this man swam across it three times every day before breakfast.'

The girl laughed when she heard this.

'Why are you laughing?' the teacher asked her angrily. 'Have I said anything funny?'

'Well, sir,' the girl answered, 'Why didn't he swim across the river four times, to get back to his clothes again?'

Word outside the 1000: ancient

A. Answer these questions.

1. Why did the ancient Romans play a lot of games?
2. Why was one of the girls interested in swimming?
3. Who swam across the Tiber before breakfast?
4. Why was the teacher angry?
5. Why did the girl laugh?

B. Do this puzzle.

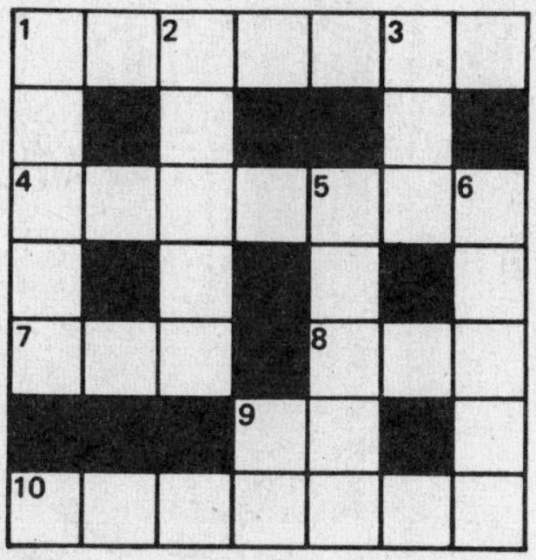

Across:

1. One of the girls in the story on page 14 was a good . . . .
4. Perhaps the famous Roman in the story ate these fruits for breakfast.
7. You want to become a good swimmer do you? Well, . . . hard and perhaps you will.
8. The ancient Romans lived two thousand years . . . .
9. The girl in this story swam . . . well . . . the Roman did.
10. The Roman . . . the Tiber three times every morning.

Down:

1. Swimming is a good . . . .
2. Rome is in this country.
3. We see with this.
5. Perhaps this grew at the sides of the Tiber.
6. Romans often fought with a 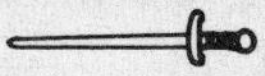 .
9. Same . . . 9 across.

C. Which of the answers to these questions are right? Write the correct ones.

1. What did the teacher in this story teach?
   a. Swimming.
   b. Games.
   c. History.
2. When the teacher said, 'Some of them swam a lot', who was he talking about?
   a. The Romans.
   b. The girls in his class.
   c. Strong people.
3. Why did the girl laugh?
   a. Because the Roman swam before breakfast.
   b. Because the Roman did not finish swimming near his clothes.
   c. Because the teacher was angry.

Word outside the 1000: puzzle

7

Betty Brown was five years old, and her mother wanted her to begin going to school, because she wanted to start working in an office again.

A month before the beginning of the school year Mrs. Brown began telling Betty about school. 'It's very nice,' she said. 'You'll play games and paint pictures and sing songs.'

Mrs. Brown began doing these things with Betty. Betty liked the games and the painting and the singing very much, but she always wanted to be near her mother, so Mrs. Brown was rather afraid and thought, 'What will she do when I leave her at school?'

But on the first day at school Betty was very good. She did not cry, and she was happy.

On the second morning Mrs. Brown said, 'Put your clothes on, Betty. I'm going to take you to school in half an hour's time.'

'School?' Betty said. 'But I've *been* to school!'

A. Answer these questions.

    1. Why did Mrs. Brown want to send her daughter to school?

    2. What did Mrs. Brown do to make Betty like school?

    3. Why was Mrs. Brown afraid?

    4. Did Betty like school when she went there?

    5. Why was Betty surprised when her mother said, 'I'm going to take you to school in half an hour's time' on the second morning?

    (Because she thought, '. . . .')

B. What words in the story on page 16 mean the opposite of:

1. nasty	4. young	7. far from
2. bad	5. after	
3. sad	6. little	

C. Write this story. Put one of these words in each empty place:

do   does   doing   make   makes   making

Our children don't . . . much homework, but they . . . a lot of work in school. My son George likes . . . furniture and things like that more than . . . lessons. He sometimes . . . nice chairs out of old boxes in his class. He and his friends . . . a lot of noise while they are working, of course.

George is good at sport: he . . . the high jump very well. Such sport . . . children a lot of good, I think. Don't you?

8

One morning Mrs. Perry said to her husband, 'Jack, there's a meeting of our ladies' club at Mrs. Young's house at lunch time today, and I want to go to it. I'll leave you some food for your lunch. Is that all right?'

'Oh, yes,' her husband answered, 'that's quite all right. What are you going to leave for my lunch?'

'This tin of fish,' Mrs. Perry said. 'And there are some cold, boiled potatoes and some beans here, too.'

'Good,' Mr. Perry answered. 'I'll have a good lunch.'

So Mrs. Perry went to her meeting. All the ladies had lunch at Mrs. Young's house, and at three o'clock Mrs. Perry came home.

'Was your fish nice, Jack?' she asked.

'Yes, but my feet are hurting,' he answered.

'Why are they hurting?' Mrs. Perry asked.

'Well, the words on the tin were, "Open tin and stand in hot water for five minutes".'

Word outside the 1000: stand (here meaning 'put it')

A. Answer these questions.

1. Why didn't Mrs. Perry want to cook her husband's lunch?
2. What did she leave him for his lunch?
3. Did Mr. Perry enjoy his lunch?
4. What was the matter with his feet?
5. What mistake did Mr. Perry make when he read the words on the tin?

B. Which of these sentences are true? Write the correct ones down.

1. Mrs. Perry wanted to belong to a ladies' club.
2. Mrs. Perry belonged to a ladies' club.
3. Mrs. Perry did not cook her husband's lunch that day.
4. Mrs. Perry cooked the lunch for her husband that day.
5. Mrs. Perry had lunch with several ladies.
6. Mrs. Perry had lunch with Mrs. Young only.
7. Mr. Perry did not like his lunch.
8. Mr. Perry liked his lunch.
9. Mr. Perry put the tin of fish in hot water.
10. Mr. Perry put his feet in hot water.

C. Write this story, but do not put pictures: put words.

Some are in the kitchen of a big

They are making lunch for a 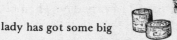 of their club. One

lady has got some big 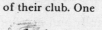 of . Another

is putting some in , and the third is

cutting some into pieces. The ladies of the club

like nice . What is *that* lady doing? Oh, she is sitting

down, because her are tired.

9

Miss Green was very fat. She weighed 100 kilos, and she was getting heavier every month, so she went to see her doctor.

He said, 'You need a diet, Miss Green, and I've got a good one here.' He gave her a small book and said, 'Read this carefully and eat the things on page 11 every day. Then come back and see me in two weeks' time.'

Miss Green came again two weeks later, but she wasn't thinner: she was fatter. The doctor was surprised and said, 'Are you eating the things on page 11 of the small book?'

'Yes, doctor,' she answered.

The next day the doctor visited Miss Green during her dinner. She was very surprised to see him.

'Miss Green,' he said, 'Why are you eating potatoes and bread? They aren't in your diet.'

'But, doctor,' Miss Green answered, 'I ate my diet at lunch time. This is my dinner.'

Word outside the 1000: diet

A. Answer these questions.

1. Why did Miss Green go to see her doctor?
2. How did the doctor try to help her?
3. Did she get thinner?
4. Did she eat the things on page 11 of the book?
5. Why didn't she get thinner?

B. Which words in the story on page 20 mean:

1. fourteen days
2. less fat
3. becoming
4. came to see
5. after that

C. Write this story. Put one word in each empty place. You will find all the correct words in the story on page 20.

Helen always ate a lot, but she never got very . . . : she was always . . . than her sister Mary, although Mary ate very little and chose her diet . . . . Helen usually . . . about 35 kilos, and Mary was always about 10 kilos . . . than her sister.

When people . . . Helen's house and saw her . . . a lot of potatoes and bread, they were always . . . and said, 'Why don't you get fat when you eat such . . . ?'

She answered, 'I don't know. I asked my . . . about it, but he didn't tell me anything useful.'

10

Rose left school when she was seventeen years old and went to a college for a year to learn to type. She passed her examinations quite well and then went to look for work. She was still living with her parents.

A lot of people were looking for typists at that time, so it was not difficult to find interesting work. Rose went to several offices, and then chose one of them. It was near her parents' house. She thought, 'I'll walk there every morning. I won't need to go by bus.'

She went to the office again and said to the manager, 'I want to work here, but what will you pay me?'

'We'll pay you £27 now,' the manager answered, 'and £30 after three months.'

Rose thought for a few seconds before she answered. Then she said, 'All right, then I'll start in three months' time.'

A. **Answer these questions.**

    1. Why was it easy to find interesting work?
    2. Why did Rose want to work in an office near her parents' house?

Word outside the 1000: manager

3. Why did Rose go to one office again?
4. Whom did she talk to there?
5. Why did she want to start working there in three months' time?

B. Put one, two or three words in each of the empty places in these sentences:

1. Rose 60%
   Sally 70%
   Judy 90%

   Rose passed her examinations well. Sally passed them . . . ; and Judy passed them . . . .

2.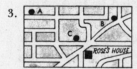

   73456 1432^2 x 245^2 $\dfrac{\sqrt[3]{543}}{\sqrt{126}}$

   x678

   The sum on the left is difficult. The one in the middle is . . . . The one on the right is . . . .

3.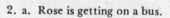

   Office A is quite near Rose's house, but Office B is . . . , and Office C is . . . .

C. Choose the right sentence for each picture. Write it down.

1. a. Rose is working in an office.
   b. Rose is studying in her college.
   c. Rose is doing an examination.

2. a. Rose is getting on a bus.
   b. Rose is getting off a bus.
   c. Rose is going past a bus.

3. a. Rose is talking to the manager.
   b. Rose is typing a letter for the manager.
   c. Rose is giving the manager a letter.

11

Mr. Day was a teacher at a school in a big city in the north of England. He usually went to France or Germany for a few weeks during his summer holidays, and he spoke French and German quite well.

But one year Mr. Day said to one of his friends, 'I'm going to have a holiday in Athens. But I don't speak Greek, so I'll go to evening classes and have Greek lessons for a month before I go.'

He studied very hard for a month, and then his holidays began and he went to Greece.

When he came back a few weeks later, his friend said to him, 'Did you have any trouble with your Greek when you were in Athens, Dick?'

'No, I didn't have any trouble with it,' answered Mr. Day. 'But the Greeks did!'

A. **Answer these questions.**

1. Where did Mr. Day usually spend some time during his holidays?
2. Why did he want to have Greek lessons?
3. Where did he go to learn Greek?
4. How long did he stay in Greece?
5. How much did his Greek help him while he was in Greece?

B. Do this puzzle.

Across:
  2. Mr. Day learnt Greek for a . . . .
  5. Mr. Day . . . , 'I'm going to learn Greek.'
  7. Mr. Day went around Greece . . . foot.
  8. It isn't easy to learn Greek: it is . . . .
  10. 'What language do the Greeks . . . ?' 'Greek, of course!'

Down:
  1. Mr. Day had Greek . . . in an evening class.
  2. Mr. Day did not walk along . . . roads in Greece: he walked along small side roads.
  3. 'Did Mr. Day have trouble with his Greek in Athens?' '. . . .'

  4. Mr. Day had a few weeks' . . . in Greece.
  6. He came . . . from Greece by train.
  9. His friend said to him, '. . . careful when you are in Greece! The girls are very pretty!'

C. Which of the answers to these questions are right? Write them down.

  1. Why did Mr. Day have Greek lessons?
     a. Because he liked evening classes.
     b. Because he wanted to visit Greece.
     c. Because he did not like French and German.

  2. How long did Mr. Day stay in Greece?
     a. A month.
     b. A few weeks.
     c. One year.

  3. What did the Greeks have trouble with?
     a. Mr. Day's Greek.
     b. Mr. Day's friend.
     c. Mr. Day's holiday.

Word outside the 1000: puzzle

91

12

Mr. Pearce liked shooting ducks very much. Whenever he had a free day, he went out shooting with his friends.

But one summer he said to himself, 'I've never been to the mountains. My holidays are going to begin soon, so I'm going to go to the mountains and shoot deer. They're more interesting than ducks, I think.'

So when his holidays began, Mr. Pearce went to the station, bought his ticket and was soon in the mountains.

He got out at a small station and walked through fields and forests for a few kilometres. Then he saw a farmer in a field.

'Good morning,' Mr. Pearce said to him. 'Are there any deer here?'

'Well,' answered the farmer slowly, 'there was one last year, but all the gentlemen from the town came and shot at it, and it's gone somewhere else now, I think.'

Word outside the 1000: deer

A. Answer these questions.

1. What sport did Mr. Pearce enjoy most?
2. Why did he want to go to the mountains?
3. How did he go to the mountains?
4. Whom did he speak to there?
5. Why did the deer go away from that place?

B. *Opposites*. Write these sentences. Put one word in each empty place.

1. Mr. Pearce wasn't free last week. He was very . . . .
2. His holidays began on the 15th of June, and they . . . on the 29th.
3. The farmer did not speak . . . : he spoke slowly.
4. When the gentlemen from the town shot at the deer, they never hit it: they always . . . it.
5. Mr. Pearce has often shot ducks, but he has . . . shot a deer.

C. Put the number of the correct sentence under the correct picture.

1. Mr. Pearce got into a train.
2. 'The deer has gone away.'
3. Mr. Pearce met a farmer.
4. Mr. Pearce often shot ducks.
5. Mr. Pearce was in the mountains now.
6. Mr. Pearce got out again.

13

Mr. Leonard was twenty-three years old and not very rich. He was not married and he lived in two rooms in a small house in a city.

Every summer, Mr. Leonard went down to the sea for a holiday. He stayed in small, cheap hotels, but he always wanted to have a clean, tidy room. He hated dirty places.

One summer a friend of his said, 'Go to the Tower Hotel in Whitesea. I went there last year, and it was very nice and clean.'

So Mr. Leonard went to the Tower Hotel in Whitesea. But there was a different manager that year.

The new manager took Mr. Leonard to his room. The room looked quite nice and clean, but Mr. Leonard said to the manager, 'Are the sheets on the bed clean?'

'Yes, of course they are!' he answered angrily. 'We washed them this morning. Feel them. They're still damp.'

Word outside the 1000: manager

A. Answer these questions.

1. Why did Mr. Leonard stay in cheap hotels?
2. What kinds of rooms did Mr. Leonard not like?
3. Who gave Mr. Leonard the name of the Tower Hotel?
4. Why was the new manager angry?
5. Where were the damp sheets?

B. Which of these sentences are true? Write them down.

1. Mr. Leonard did not have a wife.
2. Mr. Leonard's wife was quite young.
3. Mr. Leonard went to cheap hotels because they were usually clean.
4. Mr. Leonard went to cheap hotels because he did not have much money.
5. Mr. Leonard's friend liked the Tower Hotel.
6. Mr. Leonard's friend did not like the Tower Hotel much.
7. The sheets on Mr. Leonard's bed were not very clean.
8. The sheets on Mr. Leonard's bed were clean.
9. His sheets were not dry.
10. His sheets were quite dry.

C. Write this story. Put a word in each empty place. You will find all the correct words in the story on page 28.

Mr. Jones went to the sea for a holiday one . . . , and he . . . in a cheap . . . , because he was not a . . . man. At 7 a.m. on the first morning a woman came and said, 'Please get up.' Mr. Jones . . . getting up early, so he said, 'I don't want to yet. I am still . . . tired.' The woman went away, but at 8 a.m. a . . . one came and said to Mr. Jones, 'Mr. Jones, please get up. We need the . . . from your bed.' Mr. Jones still . . . to sleep, so he answered . . . , 'Why?' 'Because breakfast is starting,' answered the woman, 'and we need to put them on our tables. They're our table-cloths too.'

14

Two years after Tom and Elizabeth married, they went to live in a small flat in a big city. They were both quite young: Tom was twenty-six and Elizabeth was twenty-two. Tom worked in a bank, and Elizabeth worked in a big office.

Elizabeth always cooked the dinner when they got home, and when they had meat, Tom always cut it up when they sat down to eat.

While Tom was cutting the meat up one evening, Elizabeth said to him, 'When we were first married, Tom, you always gave me the bigger piece of meat when you cut it, and you kept the smaller one for yourself. Now you do the opposite: you give me the smaller piece and keep the bigger one for yourself. Why do you do that? Don't you love me any more?'

Her husband laughed and answered, 'Oh, no, Elizabeth. It isn't that! It's because you've learned to cook now!'

A. Answer these questions.

1. Who cooks in Tom's house?
2. What work does Tom do during meals?
3. What did Tom always do when he and Elizabeth first married?
4. What does he do now?
5. Why has he changed?

B. Which words in the story on page 30 mean:

1. arrived
2. like very much
3. into pieces
4. became husband and wife
5. made

C. Write this story, but do not put pictures: put words.

This is near a big . Hundreds of

people work in it. They bring in,

it into small , it, and then put

it in tins. One woman worked here for ten years, and then she

 a man from her . One day he

said to her, 'Why do we never a tin of meat from

your factory?' She and answered, 'I see enough

of it while I'm working!'

15

Mrs. Jenkins went to see her doctor one day, because her heart was giving her trouble.

The doctor listened to her heart carefully and did a few other things. Then he said, 'Well, Mrs. Jenkins, stop smoking, and then you'll soon be quite all right again.'

'But doctor,' answered Mrs. Jenkins quickly, 'I've never smoked. I don't like smoking.'

'Oh, well,' said the doctor, 'then don't drink any more alcohol.'

'But I don't drink alcohol,' answered Mrs. Jenkins at once.

'Stop drinking tea and coffee then,' the doctor said to her.

'I only drink water,' answered Mrs. Jenkins. 'I don't like tea or coffee.'

The doctor thought for a few seconds and then said, 'Well, . . . er . . . do you like fried potatoes?'

'Yes, I like them very much,' answered Mrs. Jenkins.

'All right, then stop eating those,' said the doctor as he got up to say goodbye to Mrs. Jenkins.

A. Answer these questions.

1. What was Mrs. Jenkins having trouble with?
2. Why did Mrs. Jenkins not smoke?
3. What did Mrs. Jenkins drink?
4. What did she like eating?
5. What did the doctor want her to do?

Word outside the 1000: alcohol

B. **Do this puzzle.**

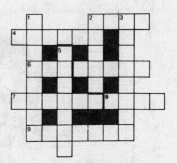

Across:

2. The doctor sent Mrs. Jenkins
   a . . . for £2.
4. Mrs. Jenkins never drank
   tea or . . . .
6. The doctor said, '. . . , then
   stop eating fried potatoes.'
   (two words)
7. Not I, not you, and not anyone else.
8. Mrs. Jenkins said, 'I . . . fried
   potatoes.'
9. I've never smoked.
   I don't like . . . .

Down:

1. Mrs. Jenkins liked fried . . .
   very much.

2. This is the opposite of
   'stop'.
3. A man burned his finger
   while he was . . . a cigarette with a match.
5. Mrs. Jenkins never drank
   this.

C. **Write this story. Choose the correct words** (to . . . or -ing):

When Helen finished { to work / working } in Iran, she came back to

England { to work / working } in a bank. She wanted a car, so I offered

{ to teach / teaching } her { to drive / driving } . She enjoyed { to learn / learning } very much,

and she learned { to drive / driving } well, very quickly. Of course, she some-

times forgot { to put / putting } her hand out when she wanted { to turn / turning },

and she did not always remember { to get / getting } petrol when she

needed it, but she soon stopped { to make / making } mistakes, and when

she went { to take / taking } her test*, she passed easily.

Word outside the 1000: puzzle   *A kind of examination.*

99

16

John liked chocolates very much, but his mother never gave
him any, because they were bad for his teeth, she thought.
But John had a very nice grandfather. The old man loved his
grandson very much, and sometimes he brought John chocolates when he came to visit him. Then his mother let him eat
them, because she wanted to make the old man happy.

One evening, a few days before John's seventh birthday, he
was saying his prayers in his bedroom before he went to bed.
'Please, God,' he shouted, 'make them give me a big box of
chocolates for my birthday on Saturday.'

His mother was in the kitchen, but she heard the small boy
shouting and went into his bedroom quickly.

'Why are you shouting, John?' she asked her son. 'God can
hear you when you talk quietly.'

'I know,' answered the clever boy with a smile, 'but Grandfather's in the next room, and he can't.'

Word outside the 1000: prayer

A. Answer these questions.

1. Why didn't John get any chocolates from his mother?
2. Why did his grandfather give him chocolates?
3. Who did John really mean when he said 'them' while he was saying his prayers?
4. Why did John's mother go into his bedroom quickly?
5. What did John want his grandfather to do on Saturday?

B. *Opposites.* What words in the story on page 34 mean the opposite of:

1. good	4. always	7. stupid
2. small	5. hated	
3. loudly	6. slowly	

C. Put the number of the correct sentence under the correct picture.

1. John said his prayers.
2. His mother ran into his bedroom.
3. John's mother did not want to spoil his teeth.
4. John's grandfather gave him some chocolates.
5. He shouted loudly.
6. John smiled and said, 'Grandfather can't hear me well.'

17

It was Jimmy's birthday, and he was five years old. He got quite a lot of nice birthday presents from his family, and one of them was a beautiful big drum.

'Who gave him that thing?' Jimmy's father said when he saw it.

'His grandfather did,' answered Jimmy's mother.

'Oh,' said his father.

Of course, Jimmy liked his drum very much. He made a terrible noise with it, but his mother did not mind. His father was working during the day, and Jimmy was in bed when he got home in the evening, so he did not hear the noise.

But one of the neighbours did not like the noise at all, so one morning a few days later, she took a sharp knife and went to Jimmy's house while he was hitting his drum. She said to him, 'Hullo, Jimmy. Do you know, there's something very nice inside your drum. Here's a knife. Open the drum and let's find it.'

Word outside the 1000: drum

A. Answer these questions.

1. When did Jimmy get the drum?
2. Whom did he get it from?
3. Why didn't his father hear it?
4. Why did the neighbour really want Jimmy to cut the drum open?
5. What did she say to Jimmy to make him cut it open?

B. Write these sentences. Put one of these in each empty place:

a lot   a lot of   many   much

'How . . . did Jimmy's drum cost?'
'Oh, it didn't cost . . . ; but his toy horse cost quite . . . .'
'How . . . other birthday presents did he get?'
'He got quite . . . nice things.'
'Did he get . . . other toys?'
'Oh, yes, he got quite . . . . And he got . . . chocolate, but not . . . sweets.'
'Did he get . . . chocolate from his parents?'
'No, he didn't get any from them.'

C. Which of the answers to these questions are right? Write the correct ones down:

1. Who gave Jimmy the drum?
   a. His father.
   b. His grandfather.
   c. His mother.
2. Why did Jimmy's father not stop him making a noise with the drum?
   a. Because he didn't mind.
   b. Because he wasn't at home then.
   c. Because Jimmy only played it in the evening.
3. What did Jimmy's neighbour really want him to do?
   a. To spoil his drum.
   b. To find something nice in his drum.
   c. To make a noise on his drum with a knife.

18

When Tom Howard was seventeen years old he was as tall as his father, so he began to borrow Mr. Howard's clothes when he wanted to go out with his friends in the evening.

Mr. Howard did not like this, and he always got very angry when he found his son wearing any of his things.

One evening when Tom came downstairs to go out, his father stopped him in the hall. He looked at Tom's clothes very carefully.

Then he said angrily, 'Isn't that one of my ties, Tom?'

'Yes, Father, it is,' answered Tom.

'And that shirt's mine too, isn't it?' his father continued.

'Yes, that's yours too,' answered Tom.

'*And* you're wearing my belt!' said Mr. Howard.

'Yes, I am, Father,' answered Tom. 'You don't want your trousers to fall down, do you?'

Word outside the 1000: tie (n.)

A. Answer these questions.

1. When did Tom begin to borrow his father's clothes?
2. When did he put them on?
3. What did Tom's father do when he borrowed his clothes?
4. Which of his father's clothes was Tom wearing in this story?

B. *Opposites*. **Write these sentences. Put one word in each empty place.**

1. Tom was not a . . . boy. He was a tall boy.
2. Mr. Howard was not . . . when Tom borrowed his clothes: he was angry.
3. Mr. Howard did not . . . his clothes to Tom; but Tom borrowed them.
4. Tom didn't borrow his father's oldest clothes. He borrowed his . . . ones.
5. Tom did not want his father's trousers to fall down: he wanted them to . . . .

C. Choose the right sentence for each picture. Write it down.

1. a. Joe is as tall as his father.
   b. Joe is less tall than his father.
   c. Joe is taller than his father.

2. a. Tom is going upstairs.
   b. Tom is coming upstairs.
   c. Tom is coming downstairs.

3. a. Tom is wearing a belt.
   b. Tom isn't wearing a belt.
   c. Tom's belt has broken.

19

Mr. Yates was nearly ninety, so it was often difficult for him to remember things, but he still liked travelling very much, so he and his wife went to Spain every year. One summer when they were there, they went to visit some friends. These people had two young daughters.

One afternoon Mr. Yates was talking to one of the girls in the garden after lunch. 'You and your sister were ill when my wife and I were here last year, weren't you?' he said to her.

'Yes, we were,' answered the girl. 'We were very ill.'

The old man said nothing for a minute, because he was thinking. Then at last he said, 'Oh, yes, I remember now! One of you died. Which one of you was it, you or your sister?'

The girl answered, 'It was me.'

'Oh? I'm very sorry to hear it,' said the old man.

A. **Answer these questions.**

    1. Why did Mr. Yates not remember things very well?
    2. Where did his friends live?
    3. Who were ill when Mr. and Mrs. Yates visited Spain another time?
    4. Who really died then?
    5. Was the girl having a joke with Mr. Yates?

B. **Which words in the story on page 40 mean:**

    1. almost   3. sad   5. stopped living
    2. not forget   4. hard

C. **Write this story. Put one word in each empty place. You will find all the correct words in the story on page 40.**

    Mr. and Mrs. Yates lived together for 52 years, and then she became very . . . . After a month she . . . , and Mr. Yates was alone. It was . . . for him to live in a big house without anybody else, so he married again. His new . . . was much younger than he was, and she liked . . . to foreign countries, so they began to go to Africa every . . . , in the winter. Mrs. Yates had a younger . . . , and she usually went with them too. Everybody thought, 'Those girls are that old man's . . . .'

    One day in Kenya a man said to him, 'Do you . . . me? I was your neighbour in Southampton.'

    Mr. Jones did not answer for a few seconds, because he was . . . . Then he said, 'Oh, yes! That's right! I married your daughter, didn't I?'

20

Mr. Knott was a teacher. He taught in a big school in London. He lived a long way from the school, so he was usually quite tired when he got home. At nine o'clock one evening, when he was in bed, the telephone bell rang in the hall of his small house, so he went downstairs, picked up the telephone and said, 'This is Whitebridge 3165. Who's speaking, please?'

'Watt,' a man answered.

'What's your name, please?' said Mr. Knott.

'Watt's my name,' was the answer.

'Yes, I asked you that. What's your name?' Mr. Knott said again.

'I told you. Watt's my name,' said the other man. 'Are you Jack Smith?'

'No, I'm Knott,' answered Mr. Knott.

'Will you give me your name, please?' said Mr. Watt.

'Will Knott,' answered Mr. Knott.

Both Mr. Watt and Mr. Will Knott put their telephones down angrily and thought, 'That was a rude, stupid man!'

A. Answer these questions.

   1. Why was Mr. Knott usually tired in the evenings?
   2. Why did he get up and go downstairs when he was already in bed?
   3. Who telephoned him?

Word outside the 1000: rude

4. Whom did Mr. Watt want to speak to?
5. When Mr. Knott said, 'Will Knott,' what did Mr. Watt think?
(He thought, '. . . .')

B. Do this puzzle.

Across:

1. The name of the teacher in this story is . . . . . . (two words).
5. 'Whom did Mr. Knott speak . . . on the telephone?' 'Mr. Watt.'
6. Perhaps Mr. Knott went to the . . . on Saturday evenings to see a film.
8. Trees and other plants grow in . . . .
10. Not yes.
11. Both men in this story . . . angry when they did not understand each other.
12. Less polite.
13. Mr. Knott went downstairs because the . . . rang.

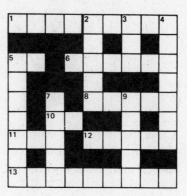

Down:

2. We cut fruit up with this.
3. In how many schools did Mr. Knott work? 'In . . . .'
4. Mr. Knott was a . . . .
5. Mr. Watt . . . , 'That was a rude, stupid man!'
7. Mr. Watt waited . . . someone answered the telephone, and then he spoke.
9. Perhaps Mr. Knott listened to the news on the . . . before he went to bed.

C. Write this story. Put *the* or nothing in each empty place.

George and Dorothy go to . . . school by . . . bus in . . . morning, but they usually come home in . . . 5.15 train. George is Dorothy's brother. He doesn't like school: when he is at . . . home, he listens to . . . radio or plays . . . trumpet, and then he is happy. On . . . Monday morning he sometimes says, 'I have a terrible pain in . . . stomach,' and he does not go to . . . school with Dorothy. His father and mother are already at . . . work, so they do not know. They go to . . . work very early. Dorothy plays . . . tennis a lot. When she leaves school, she wants to go into . . . army.

Word outside the 1000: puzzle

21

Carol Roberts left school when she was seventeen and then thought, 'What's going to happen now? I want to marry a nice, young man and have children, but no nice, young men have asked me yet. Will I meet one soon, and will he want to marry me?'

She spoke to her best friend about these questions, and her best friend said, 'Go and ask a fortune-teller. Perhaps she'll give you the answers.'

So Carol went to see a fortune-teller. The fortune-teller said to her, 'I'll give you answers to two questions. It'll cost you five pounds.'

Carol was surprised. She thought for some time, but at last she paid the money. Then she said to the fortune-teller, 'Isn't that very expensive for only two questions?'

'Yes, it is,' answered the fortune-teller. 'And now what's your second question?'

A. Answer these questions.

　　1. What did Carol want to do after she left school?
　　2. What questions did she want to ask the fortune-teller?
　　3. Why was Carol surprised?
　　4. How much money did she give the fortune-teller?
　　5. How did she spend half that money?

Word outside the 1000: fortune-teller

B. Put one, two or three words in each of the empty places in these sentences.

1. Bill is young. Peter is . . . .
   Joe is . . . .

2. The first fortune-teller is friendly,
   the second one is . . . , and
   the third is . . . .

3. The girl on the left is surprised. The one in the middle
   is . . . . And the one on the
   right is . . . .

C. Write this story, but do not put pictures: put words.

This  is a teacher in a . The small

  in his classes are very good at mathematics. When

he asks them   about , they know

all the . He says, 'One hundred are

840 French francs today. Oranges one franc

twenty each. How many will I get for one pound? Quick!' And he

is not when they all answer, 'Seven, sir! They're

rather , aren't they?'

22

Jack had a small, red car, and he liked driving it very fast. This was all right when he was out in the country, but in towns and big villages driving fast is dangerous, so there is always a speed limit. In Jack's country it was fifty kilometres an hour. Jack often drove faster than that through towns.

One day Jack was driving his small, red car through a town when a very young policeman stopped him and said, 'You were driving at more than fifty kilometres an hour, sir. Please give me your name and address.'

Jack looked at the young policeman carefully for a few seconds and then said to him, 'But I started my journey less than an hour ago!'

The policeman was new to this work and did not know the answer to Jack's excuse. He thought for a few seconds and then let Jack go.

Words outside the 1000: speed limit

A. Answer these questions.

1. Why is there a speed limit in towns and big villages?
2. How fast did Jack sometimes drive through towns?
3. Why did the young policeman stop Jack?
4. What was Jack's excuse? (He said, '. . . .')
5. Why did the policeman let Jack go?

B. *Opposites.* **What words in the story on page 46 mean the opposite of:**

1. slowly
2. wrong
3. carelessly
4. more
5. big
6. slower
7. safe

C. Which of these sentences are true? Write them down.

1. There was no speed limit outside towns and big villages.
2. The speed limit outside towns and big villages was 50 kilometres an hour.
3. Jack often drove faster than 50 kilometres an hour in towns.
4. Jack often drove faster than the speed limit.
5. The policeman wanted Jack's name and address.
6. Jack wanted the policeman's name and address.
7. Jack's excuse was a good one.
8. Jack's excuse was a bad one.
9. The policeman let Jack go because he thought, 'Perhaps that's a good excuse.'
10. The policeman let Jack go because he was new at that work.

23

Dick was seven years old, and his sister, Catherine, was five. One day their mother took them to their aunt's house to play while she went to the big city to buy some new clothes.

The children played for an hour, and then at half past four their aunt took Dick into the kitchen. She gave him a nice cake and a knife and said to him, 'Now here's a knife, Dick. Cut this cake in half and give one of the pieces to your sister, but remember to do it like a gentleman.'

'Like a gentleman?' Dick asked. 'How do gentlemen do it?'

'They always give the bigger piece to the other person,' answered his aunt at once.

'Oh,' said Dick. He thought about this for a few seconds. Then he took the cake to his sister and said to her, 'Cut this cake in half, Catherine.'

A. Answer these questions.

1. Why did the children's mother leave them at their aunt's house?
2. What did Dick's aunt want him to do with the cake?
3. What do gentlemen do when there are two pieces of cake?
4. Which piece did Dick's aunt want him to give Catherine?
5. What did Dick do with the cake?

B. Which of the answers to these questions are right? Write the questions and the correct answers down.

1. Which child was younger?
   a. Catherine was.
   b. Dick was.
2. Who wanted Dick to cut the cake?
   a. A gentleman.
   b. His aunt.
   c. Catherine.
3. Why did Dick take the cake to Catherine?
   a. Because he wasn't hungry.
   b. Because he wanted to be like a gentleman.
   c. Because he wanted the bigger piece.

C. Put the number of the correct sentence under the correct picture.

1. Dick went to Catherine with the cake.
2. Dick's aunt showed him a cake.
3. Dick went into the kitchen with his aunt.
4. Dick said, 'Cut this cake in half.'
5. The children's mother left them with their aunt.
6. His aunt gave him a knife.

24

A small boy and his father were having a walk in the country when it suddenly began to rain very hard. They did not have their umbrellas with them, and there was nowhere to hide from the rain, so they were soon very wet, and the small boy did not feel very happy.

For a long time while they were walking home through the rain, the boy was thinking. Then at last he turned to his father and said to him, 'Why does it rain, Father? It isn't very nice, is it?'

'No, it isn't very nice, but it's very useful, Tom,' answered his father. 'It rains to make the fruit and the vegetables grow for us, and to make the grass grow for the cows and sheep.'

Tom thought about this for a few seconds, and then he said, 'Then, why does it rain on the road too, Father?'

A. Answer these questions.

1. Where were the small boy and his father when it began to rain?
2. Why did they get wet?
3. Why didn't the small boy feel happy? ·
4. How is rain useful?
5. Was Tom happy with his father's answer?

B. *Opposites.* **Write these sentences. Put one word in each empty place.**

1. The small boy did not like being wet: he preferred to be . . . .
2. The boy did not think for a . . . time: he thought for a long time.
3. He thought, 'Rain isn't nice. It's . . . .'
4. But rain isn't . . . : it's very useful.
5. The boy was not . . . : he was clever.

C. Write this story. Put one word in each empty place. You will find all the correct words in the story on page 50.

   A lady and a . . . girl were getting very wet, because they were walking in the . . . and they were not wearing coats or carrying . . . . The girl did not like being . . . , so she did not feel . . . . Then they saw a star between two clouds. 'Do you know,' the lady . . . , 'that star's much bigger than our world.' The small girl . . . about that for a few . . . , and then she . . . to the lady and answered, 'Well, why doesn't it keep the rain off us then?'

A man went into a bar, sat down, called the barman and said to him, 'Give me a drink before the trouble starts.'

The barman was busy with other people, so he did not say anything, but he gave the man the drink, and the man drank it quickly. Then he put his glass down, called the barman again and said to him, 'Give me another one before the trouble starts.'

Again the barman was too busy to say anything, so he gave the man his drink and went away. The man drank that too, and then again he called the barman and said to him, 'One more drink before the trouble starts, please.'

This time the barman was not very busy, so when he brought the man his third drink, he said to him, 'What trouble are you talking about?'

The man answered, 'I haven't got any money.'

A. Answer these questions.

1. Why didn't the barman ask any questions when he gave the man his first two drinks?
2. How many drinks did the barman bring the man?

Word outside the 1000: barman

3. How did the man drink his first drink?
4. Why did the barman have time to ask the man a question when he brought him his third drink?
5. What was the man's trouble?

B. Do this puzzle.

Across:
4. The man wanted a drink before this started.
6. Before he cleans the floor, the barman . . . up the carpets like this:
7. We usually find expensive bars in important . . . in a city.

Down:
1. The trouble in a bar . . . when a man doesn't pay for his drinks.
2. The barman caught the man by the . . . of his coat and threw him out.
3. Least shallow.

5. When the man asked for his first two drinks, the barman was . . . than he was when he asked for his third one.
8. The first two times, the barman was too busy to talk . . . the man.

C. Choose the right sentence for each picture. Write it down.

1. a. This lady is in a bar.
   b. This lady is in a restaurant.
   c. This lady is in a hotel.

2. a. This man is calling the barman.
   b. This man is calling the waiter.
   c. This man is calling the servant.

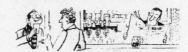

3. a. This barman is very busy.
   b. This barman is not very busy.

Word outside the 1000: puzzle

119

26

A man and his wife had a small bar near a station. The bar often stayed open until after midnight, because people came to drink there while they were waiting for trains.

At two o'clock one morning, one man was still sitting at a table in the small bar. He was asleep. The barman's wife wanted to go to bed. She looked into the bar several times, and each time the man was still there. Then at last she went to her husband and said to him, 'You've woken that man six times now, George, but he isn't drinking anything. Why haven't you sent him away? It's very late.'

'Oh, no, I don't want to send him away,' answered her husband with a smile. 'You see, whenever I wake him up, he asks for his bill, and when I bring it to him he pays it. Then he goes to sleep again.'

Word outside the 1000: barman

A. Answer these questions.

1. Why did people come to drink in the bar after midnight?
2. Why did the barman's wife want him to send the man at the table away?
3. What was he doing at 2 a.m.?
4. Did her husband send the man away?
5. Why did he let him stay?

B. Which words in the story on page 54 mean:

1. 12 o'clock at night
2. sleeping
3. place for drinking

4. more than two
5. from his sleep

C. Write this story, but do not put pictures: put words.

On some in England, there is a

Passengers go there to have a and to talk to the

 . There are no . People stand at the

bar, drink, pay their 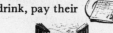 and then get out when they

reach their

At one night a woman was cleaning an empty

train when she found a man in the bar. He was ,

and there was a beautiful on his face. The woman

put the man's bag under his head and let him sleep.

121

27

Two friends were camping together. Their names were Jim and Tim. Tim was very lazy. The first evening of their holiday, Jim said to Tim, 'Here's some money. Go and buy some meat.'

'I'm too tired,' answered Tim. 'You go.' So Jim went to buy the meat.

When he came back, he said to Tim, 'Now, here's the meat. Please cook it.' But Tim answered, 'No, I'm not good at cooking. You do it.' So Jim cooked the meat.

Then Jim said to Tim, 'Cut the bread,' but Tim answered, 'I don't want to,' so Jim cut the bread.

Then he said to Tim, 'Go and get some water, please.'

'No, I don't want to get my clothes dirty,' Tim answered, so Jim got the water.

At last Jim said, 'The meal's ready. Come and eat it.'

'Well, I'll do that,' answered Tim. 'I don't like saying "No" all the time.'

A. Answer these questions.

1. What was Tim's excuse for not buying the meat?
2. What was his excuse for not cooking it?
3. What was his excuse for not cutting the bread?
4. What was his excuse for not getting the water?
5. What *did* he do when Jim asked him to eat?

B. Write this story. Put one of these in each empty place:

it was   there was   there were   they were

Jim and Tim were friends, and . . . camping. . . . September.
. . . raining, and . . . quite a lot of water on the roads, so Tim
didn't want to go and buy the meat.

. . . cold outside the tent, and . . . no chairs to sit on, so Tim
didn't want to go out and cook the meat.

. . . a lot of mud near the river, and . . . quite deep, so Tim didn't
want to go and get the water.

. . . a knife in the tent, and . . . quite sharp, but Tim was too lazy
to cut the bread.

C. Which of these sentences are true? Write them down.

1. Jim did all the work in this story.
2. Tim did all the work in this story.
3. Tim did not buy the meat because he did not have any money.
4. Tim did not buy the meat because he was tired.
5. Jim cooked the meat because Tim was not good at cooking.
6. Jim cooked the meat because Tim was a lazy boy.
7. Tim got his clothes dirty when he went to get some water.
8. Tim did not get his clothes dirty because he did not go to get
   the water.
9. Tim was not too tired to eat.
10. Tim was too tired to eat.

28

One morning a man was crossing a narrow bridge when he saw a fisherman on the shady bank of the deep, smooth river under him, so he stopped to watch him quietly.

After a few minutes, the fisherman pulled his line in. There was a big, fat fish at the end of it.

The fisherman took it off the hook and threw it back into the water. Then he put his hook and line in again. After a few more minutes he caught another big fish. Again he threw it back into the river. Then, the third time, he caught a small fish. He put it into his basket and started to get ready to go. The man on the bridge was very surprised, so he spoke to the fisherman. He said, 'Why did you throw those beautiful, big fish back into the water, and keep only that small one?'

The fisherman looked up and answered, 'Small frying-pan.'

Word outside the 1000: frying-pan

A. Answer these questions.

1. Why did the first man in this story stop on the bridge?
2. What did the fisherman do when he caught the first fish?
3. What did he do when he caught the second?
4. What did he do when he caught the third?
5. Why didn't he keep the first two fish?

B. *Opposites.* **What words in the story on page 58 mean the opposite of:**

1. thin   4. rough   7. noisily
2. ugly   5. wide
3. shallow   6. sunny

C. Put the number of the correct sentence under the correct picture.

1. The fisherman caught a small fish.
2. A fisherman was fishing in the river.
3. The fisherman threw the big fish into the water.
4. The fisherman had a small frying-pan.
5. A man was on a bridge.
6. The fisherman caught a big fish.

29

When the Americans were getting ready to send their first men to the moon, an old Irishman was watching them on television in the bar of a hotel.

There was an Englishman in the bar too, and he said to the Irishman, 'The Americans are very clever, aren't they? They're going to send some men to the moon. It's a very long way from our world.'

'Oh, that's nothing,' the Irishman answered quickly. 'The Irish are going to send some men to the sun in a few months' time. That's much farther away than the moon, you know.'

The Englishman was very surprised when he heard this. 'Oh, yes, it is,' he said, 'but the sun's too hot for people to go to.'

The Irishman laughed and answered, 'Well, the Irish aren't stupid, you know. We won't go to the sun during the day, of course. We'll go there during the night.'

Word outside the 1000: television

A. Answer these questions.

1. Who were in the bar of the hotel?
2. What was the Irishman watching on television?
3. What did the Irish want to do?
4. Why was the Englishman surprised?
5. Is the sun really cool during the night?

B. *Opposites.* **Write these sentences. Put one word in each empty place.**

1. The Irishman in this story was not . . . : he was old.
2. The Irishman did not speak . . . . He spoke quickly.
3. The sun is not . . . than the moon: it is farther away.
4. The sun isn't . . . . It is very hot.
5. The Irishman said, 'The Irish aren't stupid: they're . . . .'

C. Write this story. Put one of these words in each empty place.

at   in   on

   Pat lived . . . a farm . . . a small village . . . Ireland. He always got
up very early . . . the morning to work . . . the fields or to milk the
cows. He always had breakfast . . . the kitchen . . . 7 a.m. after
that. It was still dark then . . . winter. His wife cooked the breakfast
. . . a big stove. She did not buy much . . . the shops, but sometimes she went to the town . . . foot or . . . the bus to get a few
things. She was born . . . that town, so she always stopped . . .
several houses, knocked . . . their doors and talked to her old
friends.

30

Dave's class at school were studying English history, and one day their teacher said to them, 'Well, boys, on Friday we're all going to get on a bus and go to Conway. There's a beautiful castle there, and we're going to visit it.' The boys were very happy when they heard this.

'Now, has anybody got any questions?' the teacher asked.

'How old is the castle, sir?' Dave asked.

'It's about seven hundred years old, Dave,' the teacher answered.

'What's the name of the castle, sir?' another boy asked.

'Conway Castle,' the teacher said.

On Friday the boys came to school at 9 o'clock and got into the bus. They visited Conway Castle, and then they came back and went home.

'Well,' Dave's mother said to him when he got home, 'did you like the castle, Dave?'

'Not very much,' Dave answered. 'The stupid people built it too near the railway.'

Words outside the 1000: castle, railway

A. Answer these questions.

1. Why did the boys go to Conway Castle?
2. Who did they go with?
3. When was the castle built?
4. Did Dave enjoy visiting the castle?
5. Why didn't he like it?

B. Which of the answers to these questions are right? Write the questions and the correct answers down.

1. Why were the boys happy?
   a. Because they liked Conway Castle.
   b. Because they liked getting away from their lessons.
   c. Because they liked asking questions.
2. How did the boys go to Conway Castle?
   a. By bus.
   b. On foot.
   c. By train.
3. Why was the castle near the railway?
   a. Because people built the railway near the castle.
   b. Because people built the castle near the railway.

C. Choose the right sentence for each picture. Write it down.

1. a. These girls are studying history.
   b. These girls are studying mathematics.
   c. These girls are studying English.

2. a. This castle has got a lot of towers.
   b. This castle hasn't got any towers.
   c. This castle has got a lot of chimneys.

3. a. This castle is very near a railway.
   b. This castle is not very near a railway.

Elementary Steps to Understanding ③

L. A. Hill

Oxford University Press

外 國 語 研 修 社

Oxford University Press

Oxford London Glasgow
New York Toronto Melbourne Auckland
Kuala Lumpur Singapore Hong Kong Tokyo
Delhi Bombay Calcutta Madras Karachi
Nairobi Dar Es Salaam Cape Town

and associates in
Beirut Berlin Ibadan Mexico City Nicosia

© *Oxford University Press (Tokyo) 1980*

First published 1980
Seventh impression 1983

First Korean impression 1985
Second Korean impression 1993

ISBN 0 19 581853 9

Illustrated by Dennis Mallet

OXFORD is a trademark of Oxford University Press.

Printed in Korea

Introduction

This is the first of three new books of *Stories for Reproduction*. Each story is about 150 words long and has questions and exercises after it. This book is written at Mr. L. A. Hill's 1000-headword level. The vocabulary is given in the Appendix to this book. Some of the stories contain one or two words outside this vocabulary; these are glossed on the pages on which they appear. The grammatical structures used in these books are also strictly graded.

Other books by the same author at this same level are:
Elementary Comprehension Pieces
Elementary Composition Pieces
A Second Crossword Puzzle Book
A Fourth Reading Book
A Fifth Reading Book
Oxford Graded Readers, 1000-headword level: Junior and Senior Stories
Contextualized Vocabulary Tests, Book 1

How to use this book:
There is a cassette of this book which the student working on his own can use in the following ways (i) and (ii):

(i) He can listen to the cassette one or more times (with his book open or closed, as he wishes) and then read the story aloud himself, at first in chorus with the voice on the cassette, and then alone. After his own reading alone, he can check his performance by listening to the cassette again.

(ii) He can listen to the cassette one or more times, with his book closed, and then write down as much of the story as he can remember, and/or answer the questions and do the exercises (all without looking at the story). If he writes as much of the story as he can remember, he can then look at the story in the book, or listen to it again on the cassette, to compare what he has written with the original.

(i) gives practice in speaking with a good pronunciation, including stress, rhythm and intonation.

If the student wants to use this book for practice in understanding spoken English, he/she can use the cassette in the following ways:

(i) He/She can listen to the cassette one or more times (with his/her book open or closed, as he/she wishes) and then read the story aloud himself/herself, at first in chorus with the voice on the cassette, and then alone. After his/her own reading alone, he/she can check his/her performance by listening to the cassette again.

(ii) He/She can listen to the cassette one or more times, with his/her book closed, and then write down as much of the story as he/she can remember, and/or answer the questions and do the exercises (all without looking at the story). If he/she writes as much of the story as he/she can remember, he/she can then look at the story in the book, or listen to it again on the cassette, to compare what he/she has written with the original.

Method (i) gives practice in speaking with a good pronunciation, including stress, rhythm and intonation.

Method (ii) gives practice in aural comprehension (listening and understanding).

Other books by Dr. L. A. Hill at his 1 000-headword level are:
Elementary Stories for Reproduction 1 and 2
A Fourth Reading Book
A Fifth Reading Book
Oxford Graded Readers, 1 000-headword level: Junior and Senior Stories

Elementary Steps to Understanding 3

1

Dave worked in a factory, and he always made sandwiches in the morning, took them to work and ate them at midday.

Then he married, so he thought, 'Now my wife's going to make my sandwiches.'

On the first day, she made him some, and when he got home in the evening, she said to him, 'Were the sandwiches all right?'

'Oh, yes,' he answered, 'but you only gave me two slices of bread.'

The next day she gave him four slices, but he said again, 'Four slices aren't enough.'

The third day she gave him eight slices, but those were not enough for him either, so on the fourth day she took a loaf of bread, cut it in half and put a big piece of meat in it.

In the evening she said to him, 'Was your lunch nice?'

'Oh, yes,' he answered. 'But two slices of bread aren't enough.'

A **Which of these sentences are true (T) and which are false (F)? Write T or F in the boxes.**

1. Dave worked in an office. ☐
2. Dave always ate sandwiches for lunch. ☐
3. Dave liked sandwiches. ☐
4. Four slices of bread were not enough for Dave. ☐
5. Dave's wife gave him only two slices of bread on the fourth day. ☐
6. Dave ate a lot of bread. ☐

B **Answer these questions.**

1. Who made Dave's sandwiches before he married?
2. Who made them after he married?
3. What did his wife say on the first evening?
4. What did Dave answer?
5. What did Dave tell his wife on the second evening?
6. What did she do on the fourth day?
7. What did she ask him in the evening?
8. What did Dave answer?

C **Write this story, but put one of these words in each empty place.**

bread   butter   fingers   loaf   meat   sandwich   slice   slices

'I want to make some sandwiches.'
'Well, go and buy a . . . of . . . . Cut in into . . . . Put some . . . on one side of each . . . . Then cut some . . . up, and put some of it between each two . . . of the . . . .'
'Do I put the sides with . . . on them inside or outside?'
'Don't be stupid! Inside, of course, or your . . . will be covered with . . . when you pick a . . . up!'

2

Harry did not stop his car at some traffic-lights when they were red, and he hit another car. Harry jumped out and went to it. There was an old man in the car. He was very frightened and said to Harry, 'What are you doing? You nearly killed me!'

'Yes,' Harry answered, 'I'm very sorry.' He took a bottle out of his car and said, 'Drink some of this. Then you'll feel better.' He gave the man some whisky, and the man drank it, but then he shouted again, 'You nearly killed me!'

Harry gave him the bottle again, and the old man drank a lot of the whisky. Then he smiled and said to Harry, 'Thank you. I feel much better now. But why aren't you drinking?'

'Oh, well,' Harry answered, 'I don't want any whisky now. I'm going to sit here and wait for the police.'

A Which of these sentences are true (T) and which are false (F)? Write T or F in the boxes.

1. Harry hit an old man.
2. Harry hit another car.
3. The old man was very frightened.
4. Harry gave the old man some water.
5. The old man drank a lot of whisky.
6. Harry did not drink any whisky.

Outside the 1 000 headwords: traffic-lights, whisky

138

B Answer these questions.

1. Why did Harry hit another car?
2. What did the old man say?
3. What did Harry answer, and what did he do?
4. What did the old man do?
5. What did the old man say then?
6. What did Harry do?
7. What did the old man do and say then?
8. What did Harry say?

C Which of the two sentences (a or b) describes the picture?

1. a. Two of the lights are broken.
   b. One of the lights is broken.
2. a. The bottle is round.
   b. The bottle is square.
3. a. The bottle is full.
   b. The bottle is half full.
4. a. The sun is shining.
   b. It is cloudy.
5. a. The old man is angry.
   b. The old man is smiling.

Outside the 1 000 headwords: describe

139

3

John lived with his mother in a rather big house, and when she died, the house became too big for him so he bought a smaller one in the next street. There was a very nice old clock in his first house, and when the men came to take his furniture to the new house, John thought, 'I'm not going to let them carry my beautiful old clock in their truck. Perhaps they'll break it, and then mending it will be very expensive.' So he picked it up and began to carry it down the road in his arms.

It was heavy, so he stopped two or three times to have a rest.

Then suddenly a small boy came along the road. He stopped and looked at John for a few seconds. Then he said to John, 'You're a stupid man, aren't you? Why don't you buy a watch like everybody else?'

A Which of these sentences are true (T) and which are false (F)? Write T or F in the boxes.

1. John and his mother lived in a big house. ☐
2. John bought a small house in the next street. ☐
3. John had a beautiful new clock. ☐
4. John and his friend carried the clock to his new house. ☐
5. The clock was heavy. ☐
6. John was a stupid man. ☐

Answer these questions.

1. Why did John buy a smaller house?
2. Was it a long way from his old house?
3. Why did he not want to let the men carry his clock in their truck?
4. How did he take it to the new house?
5. What did he do two or three times on the way?
6. Why did he do this?
7. Who arrived then?
8. What did the boy say?

C **Put the right sentences under the right pictures.**

1. He did not want the men to break it, so he carried it out of the house.
2. It was heavy, so he put it down in the road.
3. John and his mother lived in a big house.
4. John bought a smaller house.
5. The men came to take his furniture to it.
6. Then a small boy said, 'Why don't you buy a watch, stupid man!'
7. Then his mother died.
8. There was a beautiful clock in John's house.

141

4

Two soldiers were in camp. The first one's name was George, and the second one's name was Bill. George said, 'Have you got a piece of paper and an envelope, Bill?'

Bill said, 'Yes, I have,' and he gave them to him.

Then George said, 'Now I haven't got a pen.' Bill gave him his, and George wrote his letter. Then he put it in the envelope and said, 'Have you got a stamp, Bill?' Bill gave him one.

Then Bill got up and went to the door, so George said to him, 'Are you going out?'

Bill said, 'Yes, I am,' and he opened the door.

George said, 'Please put my letter in the box in the office, and . . .' He stopped.

'What do you want now?' Bill said to him.

George looked at the envelope of his letter and answered, 'What's your girl-friend's address?'

Outside the 1 000 headwords: envelope

A **Which of these sentences are true (T) and which are f:**
Write T or F in the boxes.

1. George wanted Bill to write a letter for him.
2. George gave Bill a piece of paper and an envelope.
3. George got a stamp from Bill.
4. George wanted Bill to take his letter to the office.
5. Bill had a girl-friend.
6. George wanted to write to Bill's girl-friend.

B **Answer these questions.**

1. What did George say at the beginning of this story?
2. What did Bill say, and what did he do?
3. What did George say then?
4. What did Bill give him?
5. What did George ask after that?
6. What did Bill do?
7. What did George want Bill to do when he went out?
8. What did he ask Bill for at the end of this story?

C **Write this story. Put one word in each empty place. You**
all the correct words in the story on page 10.

Bill's . . . lives in London and works in an . . . . Her . . . is
Street. She gave him a beautiful . . . last summer, and he wri
her with it every week. She writes to him every week too. She
blue . . . , and then puts it in a blue . . . . Sometimes she finds
and puts that on her letter! Then everything is blue! When I
ready, she puts it in a . . . in her office, and a man takes it :
o'clock. It usually gets to Bill's . . . the next day.

5

PERSHING

MALLET

General Pershing was a famous American officer. He was in the American army, and fought in Europe in the First World War.

After he died, some people in his home town wanted to remember him, so they put up a big statue of him on a horse.

There was a school near the statue, and some of the boys passed it every day on their way to school and again on their way home. After a few months some of them began to say, 'Good morning, Pershing', whenever they passed the statue, and soon all the boys at the school were doing this.

One Saturday one of the smallest of these boys was walking to the shops with his mother when he passed the statue. He said, 'Good morning, Pershing' to it, but then he stopped and said to his mother, 'I like Pershing very much, Ma, but who's that funny man on his back?'

A   Which of these sentences are true (T) and which are false (F)? Write T or F in the boxes.

1. General Pershing was British. ☐
2. Some people put up a statue of him in his home town. ☐
3. The statue was in a school. ☐

Outside the 1 000 headwords: General, Ma, statue

4. The boys at the school always said, 'Good morning, Pershing.' □
5. The little boy was walking with his mother. □
6. The little boy thought, 'Pershing is the horse.' □

B Answer these questions.

1. Who was General Pershing?
2. What did he do in the First World War?
3. Why did people in his town put up a statue of him?
4. Who began to say 'Good morning, Pershing' whenever they passed the statue.
5. Who was walking past the statue one Saturday?
6. Who was with him?
7. What did he say to the statue?
8. What did he ask his mother then?

C Do this puzzle.

Across:
2. The name of the 6 down.
7. 'He will . . . in Europe next week' means 'He will get to Europe next week'.
8.
9. When you are . . . , you want to drink.
11. The . . . boy in the school said, 'Who's that funny man on Pershing's back?'

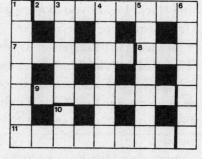

Down:
1. These are . . . .

3. Before they put the statue up, they dug a hole in the . . . and put the bottom of the statue in it.
4. More than two.
5. 'She always says to us, "Please visit my house," ' means 'She always . . . us to her house'.
6. and 2 *across:* The statue on the horse was of . . . (two words).
10. Mother.

6

Jack worked in an office in a small town. One day his boss said to him, 'Jack, I want you to go to Manchester, to an office there, to see Mr Brown. Here's the address.'

Jack went to Manchester by train. He left the station, and thought, 'The office isn't far from the station. I'll find it easily.'

But after an hour he was still looking for it, so he stopped and asked an old lady. She said, 'Go straight along this street, turn to the left at the end, and it's the second building on the right.' Jack went and found it.

A few days later he went to the same city, but again he did not find the office, so he asked someone the way. It was the same old lady! She was very surprised and said, 'Are you *still* looking for that place?'

A   Which of these sentences are true (T) and which are false (F)? Write T or F in the boxes.

1. Jack worked in an office in a large town.
2. Jack's boss wanted him to go to Manchester.
3. Jack did not have the address of the office in Manchester.
4. Jack did not find the office easily.
5. Jack went to Manchester again a few months later.
6. He asked the same old lady the way again.

Outside the 1 000 headwords: boss

B Answer these questions.

1. What did Jack's boss want him to do?
2. How did Jack go to Manchester?
3. What did he think as he left the station?
4. What happened then?
5. What did the lady say to Jack?
6. Where did he go a few days later?
7. What happened to him again?
8. Whom did he ask the way?

C There are two sentences under each picture. Choose the correct one each time and write it down.

1

a. Jack is arriving at the station.
b. Jack is leaving the station.

2

a. This office is north of the station.
b. This office is south of the station.

3

a. Jack is turning left at the end of the street.
b. Jack is turning right at the end of the street.

4

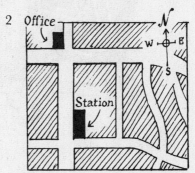

a. The second building on the left is a shop.
b. The third building on the left is a shop.

147

7

When Billy was very small, he loved pictures. His mother often drew some for him on old pieces of paper. She was very bad at drawing, but Billy enjoyed her pictures and always wanted more.

Then, when he was a little older, Billy's mother gave him some pencils and a drawing book, and he began drawing pictures too, but they were never good.

When Billy was five years old, his mother gave him a small blackboard, some pieces of chalk and a duster. He liked those very much. One day he was trying to draw a picture of his father on the blackboard. He drew lines and rubbed them out, drew more and rubbed those out too for ten minutes, but when he looked at his picture he was not happy.

'Well,' he said at last to his mother, 'I'll put a tail on it and make it a monkey.'

A **Which of these sentences are true (T) and which are false (F)? Write T or F in the boxes.**

1. Billy's mother often drew pictures for him. ☐
2. She was very good at drawing. ☐
3. Billy's drawings were not very good. ☐
4. Billy liked his blackboard very much. ☐
5. Billy drew a good picture of his father. ☐
6. Billy drew a good picture of a monkey. ☐

B **Answer these questions.**

1. What did Billy like very much when he was small?
2. What did Billy's mother give him when he was a little older?
3. What did he do?
4. Was *he* good at drawing?
5. What did his mother give him when he was five years old?
6. What did he try to do one day?
7. What happened then?
8. What did Billy say?

C *Opposites*. **Find words in the story which mean the opposite of:**

1. big
2. hated
3. good
4. new
5. sad
6. younger

8

There were men soldiers and women soldiers in an army camp, and every Sunday morning they all went to church, but a lot of the soldiers did not like it much. There was a choir of men soldiers, and Captain Jones was trying to find women soldiers to sing in it too, but none of the ones in the camp offered to do this.

Then one day Captain Jones saw a new girl soldier. She was a tall, very beautiful girl. Captain Jones went to her and said, 'Will you come and sing in the choir at our church, please?'

The girl was very surprised and said, 'But, sir, I can't sing at all!'

'Oh, that's all right,' answered Captain Jones. 'That doesn't matter at all. You don't need to *sing*: I only want someone to keep the men soldiers looking in front of them when they are in the church.'

A Which of these sentences are true (T) and which are false (F)? Write T or F in the boxes.

1. There were only men soldiers in the camp. ☐
2. There were men and women soldiers in the camp. ☐

Outside the 1 000 headwords: choir

3. There was a choir of women soldiers. ☐
4. None of the women soldiers wanted to sing in the choir. ☐
5. The new woman soldier was a good singer. ☐
6. Captain Jones wanted the women soldiers to sing. ☐

B   Answer these questions.

1. What did the soldiers do every Sunday?
2. Did they all enjoy doing this?
3. What was Captain Jones trying to do?
4. What did the women soldiers do about this?
5. What was the new girl soldier like?
6. What did Captain Jones say to her?
7. What did she answer?
8. What did Captain Jones say then?

C   Write this story. Put one word in each empty place. You will find all the correct words in the story on page 18.

Captain Jones works in an army . . . . Some of the . . . there are . . . , and some of them are . . . . There is a . . . in their . . . , and Captain Jones wants girls for it. But they do not need to . . . . They only need to look . . . . Then the men will look in . . . of them and not behind them.

Len was thirty years old, and he had very long hair. He lived in a big city, but one year he did not find any work there, so he went to a small town and began looking for work there. He went to a lot of places, but nobody wanted him.

Then he met an old friend, and this man said to him, 'People in this town don't like long hair. Why don't you go to a barber? He can cut a lot of it off, and then you can get some work.'

Len went to a barber and said, 'Please cut most of my hair off.'

The barber began. He cut and cut for a long time and then he said to Len, 'Were you in the army a few years ago?'

'Yes, I was,' Len answered. 'Why did you ask that?'

'Because I've found your cap,' the barber said.

A   Which of these sentences are true (T) and which are false (F)? Write T or F in the boxes.

1. Len was twenty years old. ☐
2. Len had very long hair. ☐
3. Nobody wanted Len for work. ☐
4. Len met an old friend. ☐
5. The barber cut off a lot of Len's hair. ☐
6. Len was in the army a few years ago. ☐

B   Answer these questions.

1. Why did Len go to a small town?
2. Did he find work at once?
3. What did his old friend say to him?
4. Where did Len go then?
5. What did he say to the barber?
6. What did the barber ask Len?
7. What did Len say?
8. And what did the barber answer?

C   Put the right sentence under each of these pictures.

1. After a long time he found Len's army cap.
2. He had very long hair.
3. He looked for work.
4. He went to a barber.
5. Len was in the army.
6. The barber began to cut his hair.
7. Then he met an old friend.
8. Then he went to a big city.

10

Mrs Robinson was a teacher in a big school in a city in America. She had boys and girls in her class, and she always enjoyed teaching them, because they were quick, and because they thought about everything carefully. One day she said to the children, 'People in a lot of countries in Asia wear white clothes at funerals, but people in America and in Europe wear white clothes when they're happy. What colour does a woman wear in this country when she marries, Mary?'

Mary said, 'White, Miss, because she's happy.'

'That's good, Mary,' Mrs Robinson said. 'You're quite right. She wears white because she's happy.'

But then one of the boys in the class put his hand up.

'Yes, Dick!' Mrs Robinson said. 'Do you want to ask something?'

'Yes, please, Miss,' Dick said. 'Why do men wear black in this country when they marry, Miss?'

A Which of these sentences are true (T) and which are false (F)? Write T or F in the boxes.

1. There were boys and girls in Mrs Robinson's class. ☐
2. Mrs Robinson enjoyed teaching her class. ☐

Outside the 1 000 headwords: funeral

154

3. The children in Mrs Robinson's class were clever and careful.
4. People in a lot of countries in Asia wear black at funerals.
5. A lot of women in America wear white when they marry.
6. Men wear white in America when they marry.

B Do this puzzle.

Across:
1. Japan and China are . . . in Asia.
6. . . . soon . . . all the pupils are sitting down, the lesson begins.
8. Dick Smith is the . . . of Mr and Mrs George Smith.
9. Dick is . . . the classroom.

10. Mrs Robinson comes to school . . . 8.45 a.m.
12. American women usually wear . . . clothes when they marry.
13. This is a . . . .

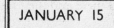
JANUARY 15

15. Mrs Robinson's pupils do not go to school . . . Sundays.
16. Not useful.
17. Mrs Robinson never drives faster than 80 kilometres . . . hour.
18. Mrs Robinson never drives dangerously: she always drives . . . .

Down:
1. Men usually wear black . . . when they marry in Europe.
2. Dick put his hand . . . to ask a question.
3. Correct.
4. Dick is . . . the classroom now.

5. Not happy.
7. The number of this question.
8. 'Did Mrs Robinson see Dick when he put his hand up?' 'Yes, she . . . him.'
11. Less fresh.
14. Yesterday was January 14th, so . . . is January 15th.

11

A few years ago, there were a lot of hijackings on aeroplanes, so now people always search passengers and their luggage at airports before they let them get into an aeroplane, because they do not want them to take guns or bombs or other dangerous things on to the plane with them.

Mr and Mrs Smith were singers, and they travelled a lot. Whenever they went by plane, people searched them and their luggage, of course.

One day, Mr Smith came to the airport, and the men searched him and his luggage first. He was ready to get on the plane. Then Mrs Smith arrived. She was late and in a hurry, but the people searched her and her bag carefully. Then Mr Smith heard her laugh and say to the men happily, 'Oh, that's very good! I've looked for those scissors for several days, and now you've found them for me! Thank you very much!'

Outside the 1 000 headwords: hijacking, search (*v.*)

A **Which of these sentences are true (T) and which are false (F)? Write T or F in the boxes.**

1. Mr Smith sometimes carried guns and bombs. ☐
2. Mrs Smith arrived after her husband. ☐
3. She was in a hurry because she was late. ☐
4. She was happy because the men searched her luggage. ☐
5. She lost her scissors. ☐
6. The men stole her scissors. ☐

B **Answer these questions.**

1. Why do people search passengers and their luggage at airports now?
2. What was Mr and Mrs Smith's work?
3. Did they travel much?
4. What happened whenever they went by plane?
5. Who arrived one day when Mr Smith was ready to get on the plane?
6. Why was she in a hurry?
7. What happened to her?
8. What did she say?

C **Write this story. Put one word in each empty place. You will find all the correct words in the story on page 24.**

Miss Jones works in an airport. Before women . . . to an aeroplane, she . . . them and their . . . to stop them taking . . . things on to the plane. Some people take . . . on to aeroplanes to shoot with, and some take . . . to throw. Sometimes women say, 'I am in a . . . ! There is no time to look in my bags! My bus was . . . !' But Miss Jones never lets them get on to the aeroplane without searching them. Has she ever . . . anything dangerous? No, she hasn't; but . . . have become very much fewer now because she and her friends do their work well.

12

Mick lived in the country, and he had quite a big garden. He grew vegetables, and he had some nice, fat chickens too. He sold the eggs and the meat, and got quite a lot of money for them.

His neighbour had a big garden too, and he also had vegetables and nice, fat chickens in it. There was a wire fence between the gardens, but it was very old, and the chickens often found holes in it and went through.

Now Mick wanted a new fence between his garden and his neighbour's, so Mr Biggs came to build it. Mick said to him, 'Please make the fence out of strong wood. And I want a hole in it. Make it big enough for my chickens to get into my neighbour's garden and eat his vegetables, but too small for his to get into mine and eat mine.'

A   Which of these sentences are true (T) and which are false (F)? Write T or F in the boxes.

1. Mick had a big garden.
2. He grew vegetables and had some chickens.
3. Mick was very poor.
4. The wire fence was old, and it had holes in it.
5. Mick wanted a strong fence with a hole in it.
6. Mick wanted his neighbour's chickens to come into his garden.

B Answer these questions.

1. Where did Mick live?
2. What did he do in his garden?
3. What did he do with his eggs and chickens?
4. What did his neighbour have?
5. What was there between Mick's garden and his neighbour's?
6. Why did the chickens often get through it?
7. What did Mick want Mr Biggs to do?
8. What did he say to him?

C Choose the correct sentence under each picture. Write the correct sentences down.

a. Mick has sold his eggs.
b. Mick is going to sell his eggs.
c. Mick is selling his eggs.

a. Mick has sold his eggs.
b. Mick is going to sell his eggs.
c. Mick is selling his eggs.

a. Mick has sold his eggs.
b. Mick is going to sell his eggs.
c. Mick is selling his eggs.

a. Mr Biggs has built the fence.
b. Mr Biggs is building the fence.
c. Mr Biggs is going to build the fence.

a. Mr Biggs has built the fence.
b. Mr Biggs is building the fence.
c. Mr Biggs is going to build the fence.

a. Mr Biggs has built the fence.
b. Mr Biggs is building the fence.
c. Mr Biggs is going to build the fence.

13

It was winter, and Mrs Hermann wanted to do a lot of shopping, so she waited until it was Saturday, when her husband was free, and she took him to the shops with her to pay for everything and to carry her parcels. They went to a lot of shops, and Mrs Hermann bought a lot of things. She often stopped and said, 'Look, Joe! Isn't that beautiful!'

He then answered, 'All right, dear. How much is it?' and took his money out to pay for it.

It was dark when they came out of the last shop, and Mr Hermann was tired and thinking about other things, like a nice drink by the side of a warm fire at home. Suddenly his wife looked up at the sky and said, 'Look at that beautiful moon, Joe!'

Without stopping, Mr Hermann answered, 'All right, dear. How much is it?'

Outside the 1 000 headwords: dear (*n.*)

A **Which of these sentences are true (T) and which are false (F)? Write T or F in the boxes.**

1. Mr Hermann did not go to work on Saturdays. ☐
2. Mrs Hermann bought the things and paid for them, and Mr Hermann carried them. ☐
3. Mr Hermann came out of the last shop and had a nice drink. ☐
4. Mr Hermann came out of the last shop and wanted a drink and to sit by the fire at home. ☐
5. Then his wife saw a beautiful picture of the moon in a shop. ☐
6. Mr Hermann offered to buy the moon for her. ☐

B **Answer these questions.**

1. Why did Mrs Hermann go shopping on Saturday?
2. What did she buy?
3. What did she often say?
4. What did he answer?
5. And what did he do then?
6. What was Mr Hermann thinking about when they came out of the last shop?
7. What did his wife say to him?
8. What did he answer?

C **This is a picture from the story on page 28, but the artist has made five mistakes in it. What are they?**

161

14

Mr and Mrs Smith married thirty years ago, and they have lived in the same house since then. Mr Smith goes to work at eight o'clock every morning, and he gets home at half past seven every evening, from Monday to Friday.

There are quite a lot of houses in their street, and most of the neighbours are nice. But the old lady in the house opposite Mr and Mrs Smith died, and after a few weeks a young man and woman came to live in it.

Mrs Smith watched them for a few days from her window and then she said to her husband, 'Bill, the man in that house opposite always kisses his wife when he leaves in the morning and he kisses her again when he comes home in the evening. Why don't you do that too?'

'Well,' Mr Smith answered, 'I don't know her very well yet.'

A Which of these sentences are true (T) and which are false (F)? Write T or F in the boxes.

1. Mr and Mrs Smith lived in the same house for thirty years. ☐
2. Mr Smith does not go to work on Saturday. ☐
3. Mr Smith comes home at six o'clock every day. ☐
4. Mrs Smith went to her new neighbour's house. ☐
5. Mrs Smith watched her neighbours from her window. ☐
6. Mrs Smith wanted Mr Smith to kiss their neighbour. ☐

Outside the 1 000 headwords: kiss (v.)

B Answer these questions.

1. When did Mr and Mrs Smith marry?
2. Does Mr Smith go out to work?
3. What are the neighbours like?
4. What happened in the house opposite?
5. Who came to live in the house?
6. What did Mrs Smith do then?
7. What did she say to her husband?
8. And what did he answer?

C Put the right sentences under the right pictures.

1. A young man and woman came to live there.
2. He comes home at seven thirty in the evening.
3. He kissed her again when he got home.
4. Mr and Mrs Smith married.
5. Mr Smith goes to work at eight in the morning.
6. Mrs Smith watched them from her window.
7. The old lady in the house opposite died.
8. The young man always kissed his wife when he left the house.

15

Mrs Peters had two children. Sammy was seven years old, and his sister Annie was four. Sammy went to school, but Annie did not. When Sammy was at home, he often played with Annie while their mother was cooking or washing or cleaning, and he was usually very nice to his small sister, and Mrs Peters was free to do her work quietly.

One Saturday morning, the two children were playing in the garden while their mother was cooking the lunch. They were quite happy until Annie suddenly began to cry and ran into the kitchen to her mother.

Mrs Peters stopped cooking and said, 'Why are you crying, Annie?'

'Sammy's broken my toy horse,' Annie answered, crying more loudly.

'How did he break it?' her mother asked.

Annie stopped crying, but did not answer for a few seconds. Then she said, 'I hit him on the head with it.'

A **Which of these sentences are true (T) and which are false (F)? Write T or F in the boxes.**

1. Sammy was seven years old. □
2. Annie was three years old. □
3. Sammy went to school, but Annie did not. □
4. Sammy was nice to his sister. □
5. Sammy broke Annie's toy horse. □
6. Annie hit Sammy with her toy. □

B **Answer these questions.**

1. What did Sammy do when he was at home?
2. Why was Mrs Peters usually free to do her work quietly when he was at home?
3. What were the children doing one Saturday morning while she was cooking the lunch?
4. What happened suddenly?
5. What did Mrs Peters say to Annie?
6. And what did Annie answer?
7. What did Mrs Peters ask then?
8. And what was Annie's answer?

C **Draw lines from the words on the left to the correct words on the right.**

1. Annie   a. broke.
2. Annie's toy horse   b. cooked the lunch.
3. Mrs Peters   c. ran into the kitchen crying.
4. Sammy   d. was nice to his sister.
5. The children   e. were quite happy at first.

16

Ted worked in a factory in a big town. He liked fishing very much, and was very good at it. Whenever he was free, he went down to the small river behind the factory and tried to catch some fish, but there were very few there, because the water was dirty. Then one summer he went to the seaside during his holidays and stayed at a small, cheap hotel.

'I've never fished in the sea before,' he thought. 'It will be rather different from fishing in our river.'

On the first day he caught a lot of fish and was very happy. He gave them to the hotel, and they cooked them for all the guests, and they enjoyed them very much. After that, he did this every day. But when Ted got his bill at the end of the week, he saw on it:

'For oil to fry fish (7 days): £3.50.'

A Which of these sentences are true (T) and which are false (F)? Write T or F in the boxes.

1. Ted worked in an office in a big town.
2. He was very good at fishing.
3. During his holidays he went to the seaside.
4. Ted caught a lot of fish.
5. He sold the fish to the hotel.
6. Ted stayed in the hotel for one week.

B Answer these questions.

1. What was Ted's hobby?
2. Where did he fish?
3. Why did he not catch many fish there?
4. Where did he go one summer?
5. Where did he stay?
6. Where did he fish there?
7. When he caught a fish, what happened to it?
8. And what happened at the end of the week?

C Do this puzzle.

Across:

1. Ted's hobby was . . . .
5. Sometimes he fished during the day, and sometimes he fished at . . . .
6.
7. Ted got his bill . . . the end of the week.
10. It is Sunday again today. He came to the hotel a week . . . .
11. Not on.
13. Ted went to the seaside to have a nice . . . .

Down:

1. When the sun is shining, we say, 'The weather is . . . .'
2.
3. Ted is getting . . . a boat to go fishing.
4. Ted was a . . . in a hotel for a week.
8. The hotel people wanted 50p for oil for . . . day.
9. 'Was the sea warm when Ted was at the seaside?' 'No, it was quite . . . .'
12. The hotel people needed oil to . . . the fish in.

MALLET

Nat lived in a small town in England. He always stayed in England for his holidays, but then last year he thought, 'I've never been outside this country. All my friends go to Spain, and they like it very much, so this year I'm going to go there too.'

First he went to Madrid and stayed in a small hotel for a few days. On the first morning he went out for a walk. In England people drive on the left, but in Spain they drive on the right. Nat forgot about this, and while he was crossing a busy street, a bicycle knocked him down.

Nat lay on the ground for a few seconds and then he sat up and said, 'Where am I?'

An old man was selling maps at the side of the street, and he at once came to Nat and said, 'Map of the city, sir?'

A   Which of these sentences are true (T) and which are false (F)? Write T or F in the boxes.

1. Nat lived in a large town in England.
2. Nat never went outside England before last year.
3. In England people drive on the left side.
4. In Spain people drive on the right.
5. A car knocked Nat down.
6. Nat wanted a map of the city.

B Answer these questions.

1. Where did Nat always have his holidays?
2. What did he think one year?
3. Where did he go?
4. What did he do on the first morning?
5. What happened while he was crossing a busy street?
6. What did he say after a few seconds?
7. What was the old man doing?
8. What did he say to Nat?

C Here is a map of a small piece of a city.

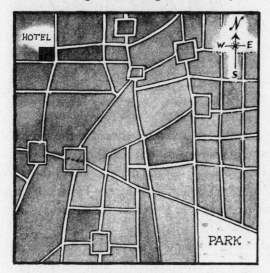

a square

1. Nat wanted to go from his hotel to the park, and one person said to him, 'Go straight south till you come to a square. Turn left in the square. Cross a second square, and then go straight on for about two kilometres. Then you will see the park on your right.' Nat went this way. Draw it on the map.

2. When Nat was walking back to his hotel, he made a mistake. He walked north from the corner of the park instead of west, and came to a square. He said to a man, 'How can I get to the George Hotel, please?' The man said, 'Go north to the next square. Turn left there and go to the next square. Go through that square to the north-west corner. Then cross the first street, and you will see your hotel in front of you.' Nat did this. Draw it on the map.

18

Harry and Bob were neighbours, and they worked in the same bank. They were young and they often went out together. Then the bank sent both of them to a new town. They did not know any other people there, so on the first Saturday, Bob said to Harry, 'There's a dance at the Bridge Hotel this evening. Let's go there. Perhaps we'll meet some nice girls.'

Bob answered, 'All right,' and they went to the dance together. They danced several times with the girls there, and then Harry went to Bob and pointed to one girl.

'She's a nasty one,' he said angrily. 'Don't talk to her.'

Bob was surprised. 'Why? What happened?' he asked his friend.

Harry answered, 'She said to me, "Do you dance?" '

Bob laughed and said, 'But that isn't a nasty thing to say!'

'She said it while I was dancing with her,' Harry answered angrily.

A **Which of these sentences are true (T) and which are false (F)? Write T or F in the boxes**.

   1. Harry lived near Bob. ☐
   2. Harry and Bob worked together till the bank sent them to a new town. ☐

3. They worked together before and after the bank sent them to a new town. □
4. They went to a dance in the new town. □
5. Bob was angry with one of the girls at the dance because she did not dance with him. □
6. Bob was angry with a girl because she said, 'Do you dance?' while they were dancing. □

B Answer these questions.

1. Where did Harry and Bob work?
2. Where did the bank send them?
3. What did Bob say to Harry on the first Saturday?
4. Where did they go that evening?
5. What did they do there?
6. What did Harry do and say then?
7. What did the girl say to Harry?
8. When did she say it?

C Write this story. Put one word in each empty place. All the words are in the story on page 38.

Harry and Bob went to a . . . at the Bridge Hotel. Harry saw a . . . and thought, 'She looks . . .' He went to her and said, 'Will you . . .?' She smiled and said, 'Yes.' They danced for a minute. Then the girl said to Harry. 'Do you dance?' Harry was angry. He stopped dancing and went to Bob. He . . . to the girl and said . . . , 'Don't dance with that girl. She said, "Do you dance?" . . . we were dancing.'

19

Mr Miller had a shop in a big town. He sold ladies' clothes, and he always had two or three shopgirls to help him. They were always young, because they were cheaper than older women, but none of them worked for him for very long, because they were young, and they did not meet many boys in a women's shop.

Last month a pretty girl came to work for him. Her name was Helen, and she was very good.

After a few days, Mr Miller saw a young man come into the shop. He went straight to Helen, spoke to her for a few minutes and then went out of the shop again.

Mr Miller was rather surprised, and when the young man left, he went to Helen and said, 'That young man didn't buy anything. What did he want to see?'

Helen answered, 'Me, at half past five.'

Outside the 1 000 headwords: shopgirl

A **Which of these sentences are true (T) and which are false (F)?
Write T or F in the boxes.**

1. Mr Miller's shop was in a big town. ☐
2. He had a lot of girls to help him. ☐
3. The girls did not stay long. ☐
4. Not many men came to the shop. ☐
5. Helen was very good. ☐
6. The young man came to buy a dress. ☐

B **Answer these questions.**

1. What did Mr Miller's shop sell?
2. Who worked there with him?
3. Why did he have young shopgirls?
4. Why did none of them stay very long?
5. Who began to work in the shop last month?
6. What did the young man do when he came into the shop?
7. What did Mr Miller ask Helen then?
8. What did Helen answer?

C **Write these sentences. Choose the correct words.**

1. Helen came $\begin{Bmatrix} \text{to work} \\ \text{work} \\ \text{working} \end{Bmatrix}$ for Mr Miller.

2. She enjoyed $\begin{Bmatrix} \text{to work} \\ \text{work} \\ \text{working} \end{Bmatrix}$ in the shop.

3. Mr Miller let her $\begin{Bmatrix} \text{to work} \\ \text{work} \\ \text{working} \end{Bmatrix}$ alone after a few days.

4. A young man came into the shop, and Helen said to him,

   'What can I $\begin{Bmatrix} \text{do} \\ \text{doing} \\ \text{to do} \end{Bmatrix}$ for you, sir?'

5. The young man wanted $\begin{Bmatrix} \text{see} \\ \text{seeing} \\ \text{to see} \end{Bmatrix}$ Helen at half past five.

20

When Jimmy was a boy, he always liked watches and clocks very much. When he was eighteen years old, he went into the army, and after a year, he began to teach himself to mend watches. A lot of his friends brought him broken watches, and he mended them for them.

Then his captain heard about this, and one day he brought him a watch too and said, 'My watch has stopped. Can you mend it for me, please?'

Jimmy said, 'Yes, sir, I can.' After a few days, he brought the watch back to the captain.

'How much do I owe you?' the officer asked.

'One pound, sir,' Jimmy answered. Then he took a small box out of his pocket and gave it to the captain, saying, 'Here are three wheels from your watch. I didn't find a place for them when I put everything back.'

A **Which of these sentences are true (T) and which are false (F)? Write T or F in the boxes.**

1. Jimmy learnt to mend watches from a teacher. ☐
2. He mended watches for his friends. ☐
3. Officers did not bring him watches. ☐
4. He mended a watch for an officer. ☐
5. He wanted the captain to pay him £1. ☐
6. He mended the captain's watch very well. ☐

B **Answer these questions.**

1. What was Jimmy's hobby when he was a boy?
2. What did he do when he was nineteen?
3. What did he do for his friends?
4. Who brought him a watch then?
5. What happened after a few days?
6. What did the officer ask?
7. What did Jimmy answer?
8. What did he do and say then?

C **Write these sentences. Choose the right words in each of them.**

 1. This watch is { breaking. / broken.

2. This bridge is { breaking. / broken.

 3. This man is { frightened. / frightening.

4. This man is { frightened. / frightening.

 5. This water is { boiled. / boiling.

6. This water is { boiled. / boiling.

21

When Alan was young, he played a lot of football, and he was very good at it, but then he went and worked in a town, and there was no team for him there, so he stopped playing.

Then he began to get rather fat, so he thought, 'I've stopped playing football, and now I'm getting fat. What am I going to do?' He thought about it for a few days, and then he said to himself, 'I know: I'll play tennis.'

He had a few lessons, and then played for a few months.

He met a nice girl at the tennis club one day, and they played a game of tennis against another young man and woman. Alan played very badly, and was very angry with himself. 'I've never played as badly as this before,' he said to the girl.

'Oh,' she said, 'you *have* played before, have you?'

A   Which of these sentences are true (T) and which are false (F)? Write T or F in the boxes.

1. Alan was good at football.
2. He stopped playing football because he was lazy.
3. He learnt to play tennis.

☐
☐
☐

4. One day he played tennis with three other people. □
5. He played very badly. □
6. The girl said, 'You have played before, have you?' □

B   Answer these questions.

1. What did Alan play when he was young?
2. Why did he stop playing?
3. What happened to him then?
4. What did he think?
5. What did he say to himself a few days later?
6. What did he do about it?
7. What happened then?
8. Why was Alan angry with himself?

C   Put the right sentences under the right pictures.

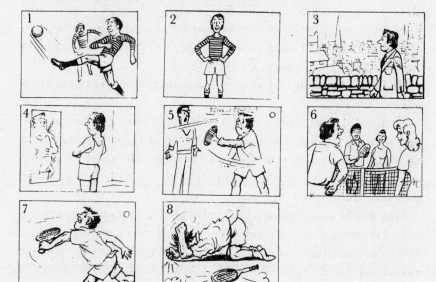

1. Alan played a lot of football when he was young.
2. He got fat.
3. He had some tennis lessons.
4. He played very badly.
5. He played with a nice girl against another young man and woman.
6. He was angry with himself.
7. He was thin.
8. Then he went to a town and stopped playing football.

22

Bruce was an Australian and worked for a newspaper in Sydney. Then he thought, 'I want to see Europe, so I'll go to England and work for a newspaper there for a few years.'

He flew to London and soon got work, because he was good at his job.

He lived in a small but comfortable house near London, and he had a small garden. He enjoyed working in it on Saturdays and Sundays. He had nice neighbours on both sides, and they often worked in their gardens on Saturdays and Sundays too, and then they talked and joked together.

One day he was digging a hole in his garden to plant a bush when one of these neighbours came to the fence between the two gardens and looked at Bruce's work. He laughed and said, 'Are you making a swimming-pool?'

'Oh, no,' answered Bruce, 'I'm going home.'

A Which of these sentences are true (T) and which are false (F)? Write T or F in the boxes.

1. Bruce worked for a newspaper. □
2. Bruce was good at his job. □
3. Bruce worked in his garden on Saturdays and Sundays. □

Outside the 1 000 headwords: job

178

4. Bruce did not like his neighbours. ☐
5. His neighbour thought, 'Bruce is making a swimming-pool.' ☐
6. Bruce wanted to go back to Australia. ☐

B   Answer these questions.

1. What was Bruce?
2. Why did he go to England?
3. Where did he live?
4. What were his neighbours like?
5. What did they often do on Saturdays and Sundays?
6. What was he doing in his garden one day?
7. What did one of his neighbours say to Bruce?
8. And what did Bruce answer?

C   Do this puzzle.

Across:

1. One day, a . . . of Bruce's said to him, 'Are you making a swimming-pool?'
6. The child cannot swim, so Bruce is . . . it.

7. Bruce dug a hole . . . his garden.
9. Bruce worked in his garden on . . . and Sundays.
11. Bruce . . . a hole to plant a bush.
12.
14. Bruce worked for a . . . .

Down:

1. Birds lay their eggs in these.
2. Sometimes neighbours . . . Bruce to have dinner with them.
3. After working hard, Bruce was . . . , so he had a big dinner.
4. One . . . Bruce's neighbours wanted to have a joke with him.
5. Go fast.
8. Women do this to their faces.

10. Less dangerous.
11. Bruce is a . . .'s name.
13. Bruce made a hole, put a bush in it, and then filled the hole . . . with earth again.

23

Dick lived in Oxford, and he had a new girl-friend. Her name was Daisy, and Dick liked her very much. One Sunday they went for a picnic in the country, and when they were walking to a nice place near a river, they saw a cow and its calf.

'Look, Daisy,' Dick said, 'that cow's giving its calf a kiss. Isn't that nice?'

Daisy stopped and looked. Then she smiled and said, 'Yes, it is, Dick. It's very pretty.'

'Doesn't it make you want to have a kiss too, Daisy?' Dick said then, looking at her.

Daisy thought for a few seconds and then she said, 'No, it doesn't really, Dick. Does it make you want to have one?'

'Yes, it does, Daisy,' Dick answered, holding her hand.

'All right, then go and get a kiss,' Daisy answered, 'and I'll wait here. It looks like a nice, quiet cow.'

Outside the 1 000 headwords: calf, kiss (*n.*)

A **Which of these sentences are true (T) and which are false (F)?
Write T or F in the boxes.**

1. Daisy was Dick's girl-friend. ☐
2. Dick liked her a little. ☐
3. They saw a cow and its calf near the sea. ☐
4. They saw two cows near a river. ☐
5. Dick wanted to kiss the cow. ☐
6. Dick wanted to kiss Daisy. ☐

B **Answer these questions.**

1. Where did Dick and Daisy go one Sunday?
2. What did they see?
3. What did Dick say?
4. And what did Daisy answer?
5. What did Dick ask her then?
6. And what did she answer?
7. What did Dick say?
8. What did Daisy answer?

C **Write these sentences. Choose the correct words in each.**

1. Daisy is a $\left\{ \begin{array}{l} \text{prettily} \\ \text{pretty} \end{array} \right\}$ girl. She looks $\left\{ \begin{array}{l} \text{prettily} \\ \text{pretty} \end{array} \right\}$ and

    dresses $\left\{ \begin{array}{l} \text{prettily.} \\ \text{pretty.} \end{array} \right.$

2. The cow gave its calf a $\left\{ \begin{array}{l} \text{nice} \\ \text{nicely} \end{array} \right\}$ kiss. She kissed her calf

    $\left\{ \begin{array}{l} \text{nice.} \\ \text{nicely.} \end{array} \right\}$ Does her calf smell $\left\{ \begin{array}{l} \text{nice} \\ \text{nicely} \end{array} \right\}$? Yes, it does.

3. It is a $\left\{ \begin{array}{l} \text{quiet} \\ \text{quietly} \end{array} \right\}$ cow. It walks $\left\{ \begin{array}{l} \text{quiet} \\ \text{quietly} \end{array} \right\}$ and always seems

    $\left\{ \begin{array}{l} \text{quiet.} \\ \text{quietly.} \end{array} \right.$

4. Whom did Dick $\left\{ \begin{array}{l} \text{real} \\ \text{really} \end{array} \right\}$ want to kiss? Did the cow give her calf a

    $\left\{ \begin{array}{l} \text{real} \\ \text{really} \end{array} \right\}$ kiss?

24

Joe and Fred were helping to build a house in a village. The weather was very warm, there was a lot of dust everywhere, and by half past twelve, they were very thirsty, so they stopped work to have their lunch. They found the nearest small bar, went in and sat down with their sandwiches.

'Good afternoon, gentlemen. What can I get you?' the man behind the bar asked.

Joe looked at Fred and said, 'Beer, I think. Yes, a pint of beer each. Is that all right for you, Fred?'

'Yes, that's all right,' Fred said. Then he turned to the man behind the bar and said, 'And I want it in a clean glass! Don't forget that.'

The man behind the bar filled the glasses and brought them to Joe and Fred. Then he said, 'Which of you asked for the clean glass?'

A   Which of these sentences are true (T) and which are false (F)? Write T or F in the boxes.

1. Joe and Fred were working in the morning. ☐
2. The weather was warm. ☐
3. They had sandwiches for lunch. ☐

Outside the 1 000 headwords: beer, pint

4. They had two pints of beer each.
5. Joe asked for a clean glass.
6. The man brought beer in two clean glasses.

B   Answer these questions.

1. What were Joe and Fred doing in the village?
2. Why were they very thirsty by half past twelve?
3. What did they do at lunch time?
4. What did the man behind the bar say to them?
5. What did Joe answer?
6. What did Fred say to Joe?
7. And what did he say to the man behind the bar?
8. What did the man say when he brought Joe and Fred their beer?

C   This is a picture from the story on page 50, but the artist has changed six things. What are they?

25

Mr Johnson was a rich old man. He lived in a beautiful house in the country with lots of servants, but his wife was dead, and he did not have any children.

Then he died suddenly, and people said, 'His servants killed him, because they wanted his money.'

But the servants said, 'No, he killed himself.'

The police came and asked the servants a lot of questions, and after a few weeks, there was a big trial. There were two famous lawyers and several important witnesses.

'Tell me,' one of the lawyers said to a witness one day, 'did Mr Johnson often talk to himself when he was alone?'

'I don't know,' the witness answered at once.

'You don't know?' the lawyer repeated angrily. 'You don't know? But you were his best friend, weren't you? Why don't you know?'

'Because I was never with him when he was alone,' the witness answered.

Outside the 1 000 headwords: lawyer, trial, witness

A **Which of these sentences are true (T) and which are false (F)? Write T or F in the boxes.**

1. Mr Johnson was a rich young man. ☐
2. He lived in a beautiful house with lots of servants. ☐
3. His wife was dead, and he had one child. ☐
4. How did Mr Johnson die? The police did not know. ☐
5. The witness said, 'Mr Johnson often talked to himself.' ☐
6. Mr Johnson was always alone. ☐

B **Answer these questions.**

1. What did people say when Mr Johnson died?
2. What did his servants say?
3. What did the police do?
4. What happened then?
5. What did one of the lawyers say to a witness?
6. What did the witness answer?
7. What did the lawyer say then?
8. And what did the witness answer?

C **Write this story. Put one word in each empty place. You will find all the words in the story on page 52.**

Mr Johnson married when he was 25. His . . .'s name was Mary. She said, 'I want to have . . . — two boys and two girls.' But then she . . . , and Mr Johnson did not marry again, so he never had any sons or daughters. When he was young, he was rather poor, but when he was . . . he became very . . . and had a lot of . . . . They worked very well for him. Then Mr Johnson died suddenly and the question was, 'Did he kill . . . , or did his servants kill him to get his . . . ?' We did not . . . , so there was a trial, and the lawyers tried to find the answer by asking . . . a lot of questions.

26

When Pat was twenty-one years old, he began to work in a small office in a city. At first he never travelled anywhere, but then he became a little more important, and he began to go to other cities for a few days to do some work there. Of course, he stayed in small hotels, when he was away from his home, but he did not know very much about living in hotels at first.

One evening when he was staying in a small hotel in Sheffield, he came back from the office and said to the clerk at the desk in the hotel, 'Good evening. Did any letters come for me today, please?'

The clerk was busy, but when he finished his work, he went to a big pile of letters and said, 'What name, please?'

'Well,' answered Pat, 'the name will be on the letters.'

A Which of these sentences are true (T) and which are false (F)? Write T or F in the boxes.

1. At first Pat did not work in other cities, because he was not important enough.
2. He stayed in hotels when he was in other cities.
3. At first he knew very little about hotels.
4. One day he asked his office clerk about letters.
5. The clerk asked him his name.
6. Pat did not tell the clerk his name.

B **Choose the correct sentence under each picture.**

1 a. Pat is at his hotel.
   b. Pat is in his hotel.
   c. Pat is on his hotel.

2 a. Now Pat is at the hotel.
   b. Now Pat is in the hotel.
   c. Now Pat is on the hotel.

3 a. Now he is at top of the
     hotel.
   b. Now he is in top of the
     hotel.
   c. Now he is on top of the
     hotel.

4 a. Pat's car is at the front
     of the hotel.
   b. Pat's car is in the front
     of the hotel.
   c. Pat's car is on the front
     of the hotel.

5 a. Pat's car is at front of
     the line.
   b. Pat's car is at the front
     of the line.
   c. Pat's car is on front of
     the line.

6 a. The name is at the front
     of the hotel.
   b. The name is in the front
     of the hotel.
   c. The name is on the front
     of the hotel.

27

Mr Reece was a farmer. He and his wife grew a lot of things and they had a few cows. They worked very hard. One day, Mr Reece said to his wife, 'Let's go to Portsmouth next Sunday. We can have a good lunch there, and then we can go to the cinema.'

His wife was very happy when she heard this, because she and her husband always ate a lot, and she did not like cooking three times a day every day.

They went to Portsmouth by train and walked about for an hour. Then, when it was 12 o'clock, they wanted to have a meal. They looked at several restaurants. In one of them there was a notice outside: 'Lunch: 12.30 to 2.30: £1.50.'

'Well, that's good,' Mrs Reece said. 'We can eat for two hours for £1.50 here! This is the place for us.'

A   Which of these sentences are true (T) and which are false (F)? Write T or F in the boxes.

1. Mr and Mrs Reece lived in a city.
2. They worked very hard.
3. They always ate a lot.
4. Mrs Reece enjoyed cooking every day.
5. They walked about in Portsmouth for two hours.
6. Mrs Reece did not often eat in restaurants.

Outside the 1 000 headwords: notice (*n.*)

B Answer these questions.

1. What work did Mr Reece do?
2. What did his wife do?
3. What did he say to his wife one day?
4. Why did this make his wife happy?
5. How did they go to Portsmouth?
6. What did they do at 12 o'clock?
7. What did they see on the notice outside one restaurant?
8. What did Mrs Reece say then?

C Do this puzzle.

Across:

5. The restaurant closed at
   . . . . (three words).
8. Somebody wrote 'Lunch: 12.30
   to 2.30: 85p' on a piece of
   . . . .
9. 'How many of the meals did
   Mrs Reece cook each day when
   she was at home?' '. . . of them.'
11. She cooked three meals . . . day.
12. Mr and Mrs Reece wanted to have . . . in a restaurant.
13. Did the people in the restaurant really let Mr and Mrs Reece eat for
    two hours?
14. Cities are usually bigger than . . . .
16. Mr and Mrs Reece looked at several . . . before they chose one.

Down:

1. These people sell things in their shops.
2. Easiest to slide on.
3. A thief has . . . my money!
4. Mr Reece always ate a . . ., because he was always hungry.
6. When Mrs Reece has a . . . in her house, she always invites a lot of
   people.
7. Less deep.
10. Mrs Reece buys her medicines at a . . .'s shop in the city.
13. The address of the restaurant was . . . 5, Smith Street.
14. Mrs Reece does not drink coffee after lunch: she drinks . . . .
15. Mrs Reece sometimes sings a . . . while she is milking the cows.
17. Mr Reece never leaves any food on his plate: he always eats it all
    . . . .

189

A 1 000-word Vocabulary

Note: This vocabulary does not contain numerals, names of the days of t
week, names of the months or proper nouns and adjectives. Not all cases
nouns and pronouns are given (e.g. *boy* stands for *boy—boy's—boys—boys*
stands for *I—me—my—mine*); nor are all parts of verbs given (e.g. *sw*
stands for *swim—swims—swam—swum—swimming*). Comparatives a
superlatives of adjectives and adverbs are also not given.

The abbreviation *a.* means adjective and/or adverb; *n.* means noun; ar
v. means verb.

a (*n.*)	arrive	because	bowl (*n.*)
about	artist	become	box (*n.*)
above	as	bed	boy(-friend)
absent (*a.*)	ask	bee	branch
accept	asleep	before	brave
accident	at	begin(ning)	bread
account (*n.*)	attack	behind	break
ache	aunt	bell	breakfast
across	autumn	belong	bridge
address (*n.*)	avoid	belt	bright
aeroplane	awake	bench	bring
afraid	away	besides	broken
after		between	brother
afternoon	baby	bicycle	brown
again	back (*a.*)	big	brush
against	back (*n.*)	bill	bucket
ago	bad (worse/worst)	bird	build(ing)
air(force, hostess,	bag	birthday	bunch
port)	bake	bite	burn
all	ball	bitter	burst
almost	balloon	black	bus
alone	banana	blackboard	bush
along	bandage	blanket	busy
also	bank	blood	but
although	bar	blouse	butter
always	barber	blow	button
a.m.	bargain	blue	buy
ambulance	basin	boat	by
among	basket	body (*and* -body,	
and	bath	*e.g. in* anybody)	cage
angry	bathe	boil (*v.*)	cake
animal	battle	bomb	camera
answer	be	book	camp
ant	beach	boot	can (*v.*)
any	bean	born	canal
apple	bear (*n.*)	borrow	cap
arm	beard	both	captain
army	beat (*v.*)	bottle	car
around	beautiful	bottom	card

careful
careless
carpet
carriage
carry
cart
cat
catch
ceiling
chain
chair
chalk
change
cheap
cheek
cheese
chemist
chest
chicken
child
chimney
chin
chocolate
choose
church
cigarette
cinema
circle
city
class
clean
clerk
clever
climate
climb
clock
close (v.)
cloth
clothes
cloud(y)
club
coat
cock
coffee
cold
collar
collect
colour
comb
come
common
continue
cook
cool
copy
corn

corner
correct
cost
cotton(-wool)
cough
count (v.)
country
course
cover(ed)
cow
cross (n.)
cross (v.)
crowd(ed)
cry
cup
cupboard
curtain
cut
cycle (v.)

damage(d)
damp
dance
dangerous
dark
date
daughter
day
dead
deep
dentist
desk
die
different
difficult
dining (-room,
  -hall)
dinner
dirty
discover
dish
dive
do
doctor/Dr.
dog
donkey
door
double
down
draw
dream
dress
drink
drive
drop (n.)
dry

duck
during
duster
dust(y)

each
ear
early
earth
east
easy
eat
egg
either
electric(ity)
elephant
else
empty
end
enemy
engine
enjoy
enough
equal
evening
ever
every
examination
except
excuse
exercise
expensive
eye

face
factory
fall
family
famous
far
farm(er)
fast
fat
father
feel
fence
few
field
fierce
fight
fill
film
find
fine (a.)
finger
finish(ed)

fire
first
fish(erman)
flag
flat (a.)
floor
flour
flower
fly (n.)
fly (v.)
follow
food
foot(ball)
for
foreign
forest
forget
fork
forward
free
fresh
friend
frighten(ed)
from
front
fruit
fry
full
funny
furniture

game
garage
garden
gas
gate
gentleman
get
girl(-friend)
give
glad
glass
glue
go
goal
goat
God
good (better/best)
goodbye
gramophone
grand- (e.g. in
  grandfather)
grass
green
grey
grill

ground
group
grow
guest
gun

hair
half
hall
hammer
hand
handkerchief
hang
happen
happy
hard
hat
hate
have
he
head
headmaster/
    mistress
hear
heart
heavy
help
hen
here
hide (v.)
high
hill
history
hit
hobby
hold
hole
holiday
home(work)
honey
hook
hooray
horse
hospital
host(ess)
hot
hotel
hour
house
how
hullo
hungry
hurry
hurt
husband

I
ice(-cream)
ill
important
in(to)
injection
ink
inside
instead
interesting
invite
iron
island
it

jam
jar
joke
journey
jug
jump

keep
key
kick
kill
kind (a.)
kind (n.)
kitchen
kite
kneel
knife
knock
know

ladder
lady
lake
lamp
land
language
last
late
laugh
lavatory
lay
lazy
leaf
learn
least
leave
left
leg
lend
less
lesson

let
letter
lid
lie (v.)
light (a.)
light (n. and v.)
like (a.)
like (v.)
line
lion
listen
little
live (v.)
living-room
loaf
lock(ed)
long (a. and n.)
look
lose
lot
loud
love
lucky
luggage
lump
lunch

machine
madam
magazine
main
make
man
many
map
marbles
marry
mat
match
mathematics
matter
meal
mean (v.)
measure
meat
medicine
meet(ing)
melt
mend
midday
middle
midnight
mile
milk
mind
minute (n.)

miss (v.)
Miss
mistake
mix
model
money
monkey
month
moon
more
morning
mosque
most
mother
mountain
mouse
moustache
mouth
move
Mr(s)
much
mud(dy)
music

nail
name
narrow
nasty
near
necessary
neck
need
needle
neighbour
neither
nephew
nest
net
never
new
news(paper)
next
nice
niece
night
no
noise (noisy)
none
nor
north
nose
not
now
number
nurse
nut

192

o'clock
of
off
offer
office
officer
often
oh
oil
old
on
once
one (*and* -one,
  e.g. in anyone)
only
open
opposite
or
orange
other
out
outside
oven
over
owe

page
pain
paint
paper
parcel
parent
park
party
pass
passenger
past
path
patient (*a.*)
pay
pen
pencil
penny
people
perhaps
person
petrol
photograph
pick
picnic
picture
piece
pile
pillow
pink
place

plant
plate
play(ground)
pleasant
please(d)
plough
p.m.
pocket
poem
point (*v.*)
poisonous
police(man)
pond
pool (*e.g.*
  swimming-pool)
poor
port
post (card,
  man, office)
pot
potato
pound
pour
pray
prefer
present (*a.*)
present (*n.*)
pretty
price
pull
punctual
pupil
push
put

quarter
question
quick
quiet
quite

race
radio
rain(y)
rat
rather
reach
read
ready
real
red
remember
repeat
rest
restaurant
rice

rich
ride
right
ring (*n.*)
ring (*v.*)
river
road
roar
rock
roll
roof
room
rope
rose
rough
round
row (*v.*)
rub
rubber
rug
ruler
run

sad
safe
sail
salt
same
sand(y)
sandwich
save
say
school
scissors
score
sea
seat
second (*n.*)
see
seldom
-self/-selves
sell
send
sentence
servant
several
sew(ing)
shade (shady)
shake
shallow
shape
sharp
she
shed
sheep
sheet

shelf
shilling
shine
ship
shirt
shoe
shoot
shop(keeper)
short
shorts
shout
show
shut
shy
sick
side
silver
since
sing(er)
sir
sister
sit
size
skirt
sky
sleep(y)
slice
slide
slip(pery)
slow
small
smell
smile
smoke
smooth
snake
snow
so
soap
sock
soft
soldier
some
sometimes
son
song
soon
sorry
soup
sour
south
speak
spell
spend
spill
spoil

193

spoon(ful)
sport
spring (*n.*)
square
stain
stairs (*also*
  -stairs, *e.g. in*
  upstairs)
stale
stamp
stand
star
start
station
stay
steal
steep
step
stick (*n.*)
sticky
still
sting
stocking
stomach
stone
stop
storm(y)
story
stove
straight
strange
street
string
strong
student
study
stupid
such
suddenly
sugar
sum
summer
sun(ny)
surprised
sweep
sweet
swim(mer)
sword

table
tail
take

talk
tall
tame
tank
tap
taste
tea
teach(er)
team
tear (*v.*)
telegram
(tele)phone
tell
temple
tennis
tent
terrible
than
thank
that/those
the
theatre
then
there
they
thick
thief
thin
thing (*also* -thing
  e.g. in nothing)
think
thirsty
this/these
through
throw
ticket
tidy
tie (*v.*)
tiger
till
time
tin
tired
to
today
together
tomorrow
tongue
tonight
too
tooth
top

towards
towel
tower
town
toy
train (*n.*)
travel
tree
trip
trouble
trousers
truck
true
try
turn
twice
type (*v.*)
typist

ugly
umbrella
uncle
under
understand
university
until
up
useful
useless
usually

valley
van
vegetable
very
village
visit(or)
volley-ball
voyage

wait
wake
walk(ing-stick)
wall
want
warm
wash
watch (*n.*)
watch (*v.*)
water
wave
way

we
weak
wear
weather
week
weigh
well (*a.*)
west
wet
what
wheel
when(ever)
where (*also* -where,
  e.g. in *nowhere*)
which
while
white
who
why
wide
wife
wild
will (*v.*)
win
wind(y)
window
wing
winter
wipe
wire
with(out)
woman
wood
wool
word
work
world
write
wrong

yard
year
yellow
yes
yesterday
yet
you
young

zoo

Oxford 대학출판부/외국어연수사간 (한국내 판권 : 외국어연수사에서 보유)
ESL/EFL 교재 저술의 세계적 권위 L.H.Hill 박사의 명저

Stories for Reproduction Series 1~4

이야기의 재현(再現)을 통해 배우는 영어1~4집

■흥미진진한 이야기를 읽거나 듣고 말과 글로 다시 표현해 보는 연습을 통해 표현력(作文 · 會話) · 이해력(讀解 · 聽解)을 획기적으로 향상시키는 교재

● 이미 40여권의 ESL/EFL(English as a Second/Foreign Language) 교재 저술로 세계적 명성을 떨치고 있는 Leslie A. Hill 박사가 그의 오랜 연구와 교육자로서의 경험을 토대로 최근에 집대성한 영어학습교재의 결정판.

● Hill 박사 특유의 Contextualized Approach(문맥적 접근법)에 토대를 둔 다양한 Oral /Written Reproduction Questions & Exercises(구두 / 필기재현연습)로 표현력과 이해력의 획기적 향상.

● A. S. Hornby 의 Guide to Patterns & Usage in English(25 구문 유형)에 토대를 두고 단어와 구문의 난이도에 따라 상용 기본단어를 4 단계(입문, 초급, 중급, 상급)로 나누어 익히고 활용시키는 교재 총서.

● 영어 실력이 약한 경우는 기초실력 재확립용으로, 어휘력 · 문법실력이 앞선 경우는 속독력 · 청해력 · 작문력 · 회화력 향상용으로 쓸 수 있는 교재.

● 교실수업, 자습 양용으로 쓸 수 있으며 자습의 경우를 위해 상세하고 친절한 주석과 해답이 담긴 Study Guide와 Answer Key를 마련.

■대학입시 · 취직시험 · 각종고시 · TOEFL 등 각종 영어 시험 준비용으로 최적.

제 1 집 Introductory, Elementary, Intermediate Advanced Stories for Reproduction 1
　　　　 전 4권 Textbook＋Study Guide＋Cassette Pack.

제 2 집 Introductory, Elementary, Intermediate, Advanced Stories for Reproduction 2
　　　　 전 4권 Textbook＋Answer Key＋Cassette Pack.

제 3 집 Introductory, Elementary, Intermediate, Advanced Steps to Understanding
　　　　 전 4권 Textbook＋Answer Key ＋Cassette Pack.

제 4 집 Elementary, Intermediate, Advanced Stories for Reproduction, American
　　　　 Series 전 3권 Textbook＋Answer Key＋Cassette Pack.

미국 영어회화의 최고봉을 정복하는
OXFORD AMERICAN ENGLISH COURSE

JACK C. RICHARDS DAVID BYCINA

PERSON TO PERSON
Communicative Speaking and Listening Skills

© Oxford University Press, Book 1, 1984; Book 2, 1985

교재 구성 : Book1 : Student Book 1권, 자습서 1권, 테잎 6개
Book2 : Student Book 1권, 자습서 1권, 테잎 6개

1 OXFORD가 특별히 한국과 일본 영어학도들의 취약점을 연구한 끝에 Communicative Speaking & Listening Skills 연마에 역점을 두고 개발한 Best Seller로 大學生/ 一般成人用의 영어회화 최종완성 Course.

2 각 Unit마다 1. Presentation Dialogue〔대화〕 2. Give It A Try〔연습〕 3. Listen to This〔청취〕로 나누어, 전 30 Units에 걸쳐 110종의 다양한 Topics를 148 종의 Communicative Function으로 엮은 Functional Course의 결정판.

3 Stress(강세), Intonation(음조) 및 Rhythm(음률) 등 초분절음소의 철저한 학습과 Communicative Skills 습득에 필수적인 특수 구문 및 어법의 집중 훈련에 주안점을 둔 새로운 교재.

4 실용/학술의 각국면을 생생하게 연출하여 12개의 Cassette에 압축한 입체음향 교재로 Communicative Speaking은 물론, Tasks, Note—taking, Gap—filling, Dialogue Completion 및 Multiple Choice 등의 연습을 통하여 구미 유학에 지장이 없는 청취력을 양성하는 Course로 TOEFL, 취직시험 등 각종 영어시험 대비용으로도 최적.

연락처 ◥ 한국내 총판 : (주) 외국어연수사

서울特別市 永登浦區 汝矣島洞35-2(白象빌딩1006號) ☎ 785-0919. 785-1749

단시일내에 미국 본토인의 빠른 대화
청취에 적응할 수 있는 최신
청취력 개발 코오스

Listen for It
Task-based American English Listening Course

영자 신문은 읽을수 있는데, <u>AFKN</u> 방송은 이해가 안가는 분, TOEFL이나 TOEIC의 Listening Comprehension 성적이 향상되지 않는 분, 미국인 교수의 강의를 거의 알아 듣지 못하는 분은 처음부터 이 교재로 빠른 대화 듣기 적응훈 련을 받으면 단시일내에 고민이 해결될 것입니다.

고교 상급반이나 대학생들은 선배들의 전철을 밟지 말고 지금부터 이 교재로 청취 훈련을 받으면 선배들처럼 시간을 낭비하지 않고 빠른 시일내에 미국인과 의 대화는 물론 미국인 교수의 강의를 들을 수 있는 확고한 기초가 생길 것입니 다.

이 교재는 일상적 관심사를 화제(topic)로 삼아 미국인들이 다양한 기능 (function)으로 이야기하는 대화에 토대를 두고 있기 때문에 그대로 일상회화에 응용할 수 있읍니다.

이 교재는 <u>고등학교 상급반이나 대학 또는 성인영어회화 과정에 적합하도록 다음과 같이 4부로 꾸며져 있읍니다.</u>

Starting out : 화재를 소개하고 대화의 배경을 이루는 정보를 제공하며 대화를 이해 하는데 필요한 표현(낱말·숙어 등)을 설명.
Listening for : 화제(topic)와 관련된 몇 가지의 과제 해결에 토대를 둔 청취 활 동.
Trying it out : 실제로 회화에 응용해서 말해보는 활동.

이 교재를 자력으로 공부하고자 하는 분들은 녹음대본과 설문의 해답이 수록 된 별책 자습서를 이용하면 좋을 것입니다.

총판 : (株)外國語研修社
서울시 영등포구 여의도동 35-2
백상빌딩 1006호
Tel : 785-0919, 785-1749

교재의 구성 : Student Book : 1권 자습서 : 1권 Tape : C-60 8개

주석·증보판

PRACTICE WITH IDIOMS
영어 숙어 연습

Ronald E. Fear 원저
李 澄 載 譯編

〈특 장〉

◉ 영어 숙어의 뜻과 구문 지식을 체계적으로 습득하기 위한 중-상급 수준의 영어 학습 교재이다.

◉ 복잡 다단한 영어 숙어를 16종의 구문 유형으로 분류하고 각 유형에 속하는 숙어로 연습문제를 구성하여 그것들을 문맥적으로 이해하는 과정에 학습자를 참여시킨 다음 숙어의 정의(定義), 연어법(連語法) 및 예문(例文)을 소개하는 귀납적 문제 해결 방법으로 꾸며놓았다.

◉ 각 장의 「숙어의 해설(Explanation of the Idioms)」항에는 숙어의 정의(Definition)와 연어법(Collocation) 그리고 예문(Sample Sentences)이 수록되어 있는데, 이 한국어 주석·증보판에서는 이것들을 대폭 증보한 후 그 번역과 주석을 붙여 놓아 영어 실력이 약한 중급 수준 이하의 학습자에게도 도움이 되도록 배려하였다.

◉ 제17장 부록에는 숙어의 이해에 필요한 문법용어의 설명과 16종의 숙어 구문형을 도해와 예문을 통해 일목요연하게 설명하는 동시에 그 용법에 대한 유의 사항도 덧붙여 놓았는데, 이 장은 전문이 한국어로 번역되어 있다.

◉ 각장의 연습문제에 대한 해답을 제시하고, 이 책에서 다룬 숙어들의 적절한 예문들을 각종 문헌과 사전들에서 골라 한국어 번역문과 주석을 붙여 별책으로 꾸며놓았다.

연락처 ＼ 한국내 판권보유 : (주) 외국어연수사

서울特別市 永登浦區 汝矣島洞35-2(白象빌딩1006號) ☎ 785-0919. 785-1749

서강대학교 영어교육연구소 연구협찬/(주) 외국어연수사 간

Common Problems in KOREAN ENGLISH
한국식 영어의 허점과 오류

이 책의 목적은 한국식 영어의 허점과 오류를 바로 잡아주고 「자연스럽고 (natural), 적응성이 풍부하며(flexible), 관용적인(idiomatic)」 영어 표현을 익히도록 하려는 것이다. 그러므로 이 책은 영어를 자주 써야하는 분들이나 각급학교 영어선생님들과 올바른 영어 표현을 익히고자 하는 학생들에게 유익한 참고서나 길잡이가 될 것이다.

특 색

- 한국식 영어 특유의 오용 사례를 정선한 후 그 원인을 밝혀내어 상세히 설명하고 올바른 표현법을 구체적으로 예시하였다.
- 오용 사례를 (1) 문법적 오류 (2) 낱말 뜻의 혼동 (3) 어색하거나 부적절한 표현의 3편으로 나누어 그 잘못을 지적하고 올바른 문장으로 고쳐 놓았으며, 그 대안으로 다양한 표현방법을 풍부한 예문으로 제시했을 뿐 아니라 방대한 연습문제를 만들고 그 모범답안까지 제시해 두었다.
- 내용설명은 물론 예문과 대화례(sample sentences and dialogs) 등이 저자 특유의 간명한 필치로 씌어져 있어 이해하기 쉽고 활용도 용이하다.
- 각 문제점의 요점을 간추려 우리말로 옮겨 놓았으며 교실 수업과 자습 양용에 적합하도록 만들었다.

저 자

David Kosofsky는 The University of Maryland에서 서양사를 전공했고(B.A.) Brandeis University에서 비교 역사학을 전공했으며(M.A.) 미국, 일본 및 말레이지아에서 영어를 가르쳤고 1982년에 내한한 이래 서강대학교 영어교육연구소에서 Advanced Seminar Class를 가르치면서 영어학습교재의 연구개발에 전념하고 있다. 현재 외국어대학교 영어과 교수. 그는 The Asian Wall Street Journal과 Asiaweek에 기고하면서 소설도 써 왔다.

최신간 AMERICAN ENGLISH Course

EAST WEST (1~3권)
© Oxford University Press 1989

3단계 과정(3권)으로 구성된 EAST-WEST는 중─상급 수준의 성인용 영어회화 과정
으로서 의사 소통 기능의 향상을 주목적으로 개발된 것이다. 문법, 기능, 주제, 상황 등
을 골고루 통합한 이상적 교수요목(syllabus)에 토대를 두고 있어, 이 교재는, 의사 소
통 능력 향상을 위하여 용의 주도하게 통제된 학습 활동을 통하여, 말하고 듣는 연습을
철저히 할 수 있도록 꾸며져 있다.

특 장

1 모든 영어 회화 교육에 적합하나 특히 말하기를 꺼리는 학생들에게나 학생수가 많은
   경우에 크게 도움이 된다.
2 전 교과를 통해서 자연스런 언어를 사용했으나, 이와 다르거나 대안으로 쓰일 표현
   도 유의 했다.
3 미국 생활의 여러 국면을 소개하기 위해 culture capsules 란을 두었다.
4 학생들의 관심을 끌고, 생활 체험을 이용하며, 솔선하여 말을 하도록 유도하는 의사
   소통 중심의 교재이다.
5 언어의 내용을 반복하면서 회화력을 육성하는 과정과 과제를 푸는 과정에서 학생들
   에게 필요한 여러가지 도움을 주고 있다.
6 두 사람이나 소집단의 역할놀이와 빈칸에 적합한 말을 넣는 연습문제들이 광범하게
   사용되었다.

단원의 구성

● 총 14단원으로 구성되어 있는 총천연색의 학생용 교재는 각 단원의 8쪽씩으로 되어
  있다.
● 각 단원은 각 단원의 교수 요점을 소개하는 대화로 시작된다.
● 다음 4쪽에는 발음 연습을 포함하여 정확성과 유창성의 향상을 노리는 말하는 연습
  이 따른다.
● 다음에는 문법상의 요점, 상황에 맞는 표현, 기능〔목적〕및 개념에 적합한 표현과
  각 단원에 쓰인 숙어적 표현등을 요약하는 Checklist 란이 있다.
● 마지막 두쪽은 수동적 기능인 청취력과 독해력을 향상시키기 위한 것이다.
● 제 1권에는 Moon of India라는 추리 소설을 14편으로 나누어 각 단원마다 실어 독
  자의 흥미를 유발하고 독서의 즐거움을 맛보게 해 준다.
● East West 는 각 권마다 학생용의 교재 및 연습장, 교사용 교재와 카셋트로 되어 있
  다. 별도로 Moon of India 의 카셋트도 있다.

판매대행 : **(주) 외국어연수사**

서울 영등포구 여의도동 35-2 백상빌딩 1006호
☎ 785-0919, 1749, 780-2817

최신간 AMERICAN ENGLISH Course

ON COURSE (1~2권)

© Oxford University Press 1989

■ 2단계로 되어 있는 **On Course**는 초급-중급 수준의 성인용 영어 회화 과정으로서 **말하고 듣는** 기능을 중심으로 꾸며진 편리한 교재이다.

■ 학생용 교재는 **30단원**으로 구성되어 있는데 각 단원은 2쪽씩이다. 그래서 사용하기가 아주 편리하며 **50분간**에 학습을 마칠 수 있도록 꾸며져 있다.

■ 또한 학생 상호간의 연습 기회를 제공하기 위하여 두 사람이 **역할놀이**를 하는 것과 빈칸에 알맞는 말을 넣어 대화를 완성하는 **연습문제**가 마련되어 있다.

■ 그리고 5단원씩 묶어서 요약하여 연습하는 총 24쪽의 6개 **요약단원 (Summary Units)**이 있는데, 이것들은 30단원에 걸쳐 제시된 재료와 자연스럽게 재 결합하여 이를 보강해 준다.

■ 각 요약 단원마다 **청취력 향상**을 위한 과제 중심의 **연습 문제**가 수록되어 있다.

판매대행 : (주)외국어연수사
서울 영등포구 여의도동 35-2
백상빌딩 1006호
☎ 785-0919, 1749, 780-2817

SMALL TALK
OXFORD UNIVERSITY PRESS 1986.CAROLYN GRAHAM저
Cassette 2개, 교재 1권으로 미국영어 특유의 발음을 Jazz Chant로 배우는 최신간

　그릇된 발음으로 영어를 배운 기간이 길면 길수록 그것이 영어 청취력과 회화력 향상에 큰 장애가 된다는 것은 ESL/EFL 교사들 모두가 통감하고 있는 사실이다. 이 문제를 근본적으로 해결하려는 시도에서 마련된 것이 이 교재이다.

　이 교재는 미국영어의 정확한 발음, 특히 강세(Stress), 음조(Intonation), 음률(Rhythm)과 연음(Blending)및 축약음(Contraction)의 학습에 중점을 두고 있다.
　특히 본문의 대화(Dialog)를 Jazz 노래가락으로 만들어 녹음해 놓았기 때문에 노래를 배우듯이 이것을 따라 부르다 보면 자신도 모르게 Native Speaker와 같은 회화력을 습득할 수 있다.

　이 교재는 주로 한국어·일본어 등과 같은 **음절어(Syllabic Language)**를 쓰는 국민들이 **음률어(Rhythmic Language)**인 영어의 정확한 발음 특히 음조, 강세, 음률등을 습득하는데 경이적인 효과를 나타내고 있어 전세계 영어 교육계의 주목을 끌고 있다.

Cassette 1
　세계적으로 유명한 Jazz 음악가들이 연주한 Jazz 음악을 배경으로 교재 본문이 노래가락으로 녹음되어 있다.

Cassette 2
　Cassette 1의 본문을 응용한 다양한 청취 연습과 Word Puzzle로 된 흥미 진진한 청취 연습 문제가 수록되어 있다.

　저자 Carolyn Graham은 New York University의 교수로서 The American Language Insti-tute에서 ESL(English as a second language)을 가르치고 있으며 Jazz를 활용한 Jazz Chants(1978), Jazz Chants for Children(1979), 및 The Electric Elephant(1982)등의 영어회화 교재를 저술한바 있다.

한국내총판 : (주)외국어연수사

David Kosofsky 저　(주)외국어연수사 발행

LANGUAGE FROM THE BODY

발상과 어원에 따라 쉽게 풀어쓴 **영어숙어**

신체언어를 중심으로

중성적이고 무미건조한 사전의 정의에 향신료와 방향을 첨가해서 언어의 표현을
한층 다채롭고 풍부하게 만들어 주는 것이 숙어이다. 그러나 숙어는 그것이 형성된 원류(源流)와
배경을 이해하지 못하면 그 참뜻을 알 수 없기 때문에, 외국어를 공부하는 사람에게는 숙어가
마치 히말라야의 미답 산봉우리들처럼 정복하기 힘들게 느껴진다.
숙어의 희랍어 어원 'idio-'가 '독특한(peculiar)' 또는 '개별적인(separate)'이란 뜻이듯이,
숙어는 그 성질상 너무 '독특하고' '개별적'이어서 그것들을 일반원칙으로 체계화해서 설명한다는
것은 거의 불가능에 가까운 노릇이다. 아직까지 영어숙어를 체계적으로 정연하게 가르치는 방법이
개발되지 못하고 있는 까닭은 바로 이점 때문이다. 그러나 이러한 영어숙어들도 그 원류를 따라
어원과 발상을 따져보고 그것이 연상, 유추, 확대 적용되는 배경을 살펴보면, 영어숙어의 체계적
인 해설이 어느 정도는 가능할 것이다. 이책은 전술한 새로운 접근법에 따라 **David Kosofsky**
교수가 처음으로 시도한 영어숙어의 체계적 해설서이다.

특 색

1. 이책에는 신체언어(**Language from the Body**)에서 유래한 700개의 숙어표현을 골라, 그것들을
   Head부터 **Shoulder**까지 27장으로 나누어 설명했다. 신체언어에서 유래한 숙어를 선택한 것은
   그것들이 영어숙어 표현의 대종을 이루고 있을 뿐 아니라 비영어사용국민으로서는 가장 이해하기
   어려운 표현이기 때문이다.
2. 각 장마다 (1)대화편 (2)해설편으로 나누었다. 해설편에서는 숙어의 어원과 발상을 따져 그 뜻을
   풀이했으며 또한 그 숙어를 이용한 많은 예문을 제시하였다. 특히, 대화편에서는 해설편에 나오는
   주요숙어를 총망라하여 저자 특유의 유머와 소설가다운 필치로 흥미진진한 대화를 꾸며놓았다.
3. 권말에 각 장별로 이 숙어를 익히기 위한 연습문제와 해답을 수록해 두었다.
4. 대화편과 해설편을 번역하여 대역판으로 꾸밈으로써 영어독해력이 약한 독자들도 이 책을 이용하
   는데 지장이 없도록 하였다.

저 자

David Kosofsky는 **The University of Maryland**에서 서
양사를 전공했고(**B.A.**) **Brandeis University**에서 비교 역사
학을 전공했으며(**M.A.**) 미국, 일본 및 말레이지아에서 영어
를 가르쳤고 1982년에 내한한 이래 서강대학교 영어교육연구
소에서 **Advanced Seminar Class**를 가르치면서 영어학습교
재의 연구개발에 전념하고 있다. 현재 외국어대학교 영어과 교수.
그는 **The Asian Wall Street Journal**과 **Asiaweek**에 기고
하면서 소설도 써 왔다.

🌐 **외국어연수사** Tel: 785-0919, 1749;Fax:780-2817

서울 영등포구 여의도동 35-2 백상빌딩 1006 호

만 화 영 어

만화를 즐기며 연마하는 영어 회화·작문 교재

English through Cartoons

Dialogues, Stories & Questions

유우머와 **기지**가 넘치는 **만화**를 즐기면서

(A) **대화**(Dialogues)를 읽거나 테이프를 듣고 영어 특유의
    유우머 감각을 몸에 익히며

(B) 만화를 해설하는 **이야기** (Stories)를 공란을 메우면서 완성하는
    연습을 통해 **작문력**을 기르고

C) 만화내용의 **질의 응답**을 통해 격조 높은 영어 **회화력**을
    양성하는 영작문·회화 연습 교재의 결정판 /

● EFL/ESL (English as a Foreign/Second Language) 교재 저술의 세계적 권위
  Leslie A. Hill 박사와 세계적인 만화가 **D. Mallet** 의 최신 역작.

● 폭소와 홍소를 자아내게 하면서도 깊은 뜻을 담은 만화와 대화는 학습상의 긴장을
  덜어 주며 Stories 의 공란을 추리하여 완성토록 유도하는 연습문제와 내용 파악
  질의문은 영어의 회화력·청취력·작문력·독해력을 획기적으로 연마·향상.

● 학습 부담을 줄이고 능률을 최대한으로 올리기 위하여 친절하고 자세한 해설과 예문이
  풍부하게 수록된 **Study Guide** 를 따로 마련.

저자소개

L. A. Hill 박사는 ELT(English Language Teaching) 교재의 저술가로서 그리고 영어 교육계의 세계적인 권위자로 널리 알려진 분으로 그의 저서에는 다음과 같은 것들이 있다.
Stories for Reproduction 1 (전 4 권), Stories for Reproduction 2 (전 4 권), Stories for Reproduction: American Series(전 3 권), Steps to Understanding (전 4 권), Word Power 1500/3000/4500 (전 3 권), English through Cartoons(전 2 권), Elementary & Intermediate Composition Pieces(전 2 권), Elementary & Intermediate Comprehension Pieces(전 2 권), Intermediate Comprehension Topics, Oxford Graded Readers(전 4 권), Writing for a Purpose, Note-taking Practice, A Guide to Correct English & Exercises (전 2 권), Prepositions & Adverbial Particles & Exercises(전 2 권), Contextualized Vocabulary Tests (전 4 권), Crossword Puzzle Book(전 4 권).

Elementary Stories for Reproduction 1-3

1985년 2월 12일 발   행
1993년 2월 20일 합본 1 쇄

지은이   L. A. HILL
펴낸이   李 瀅 載
펴낸곳   外國語研修社

판권
본사
소유

서
등
전
FA